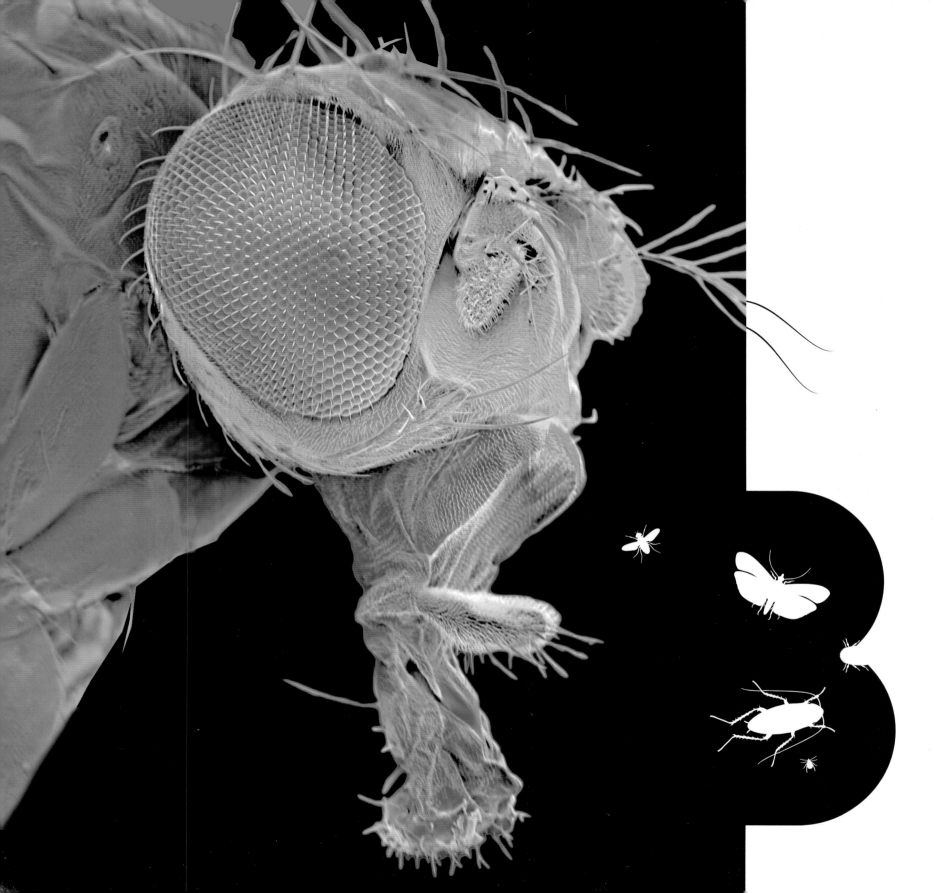

Entomologist Bert Hölldobler of the University of Würzburg in Germany examines *Camponotus sericeiventris,* a neotropical forest-dwelling species of carpenter ant.

BUZZ   THE INTIMATE BOND BETWEEN HUMANS AND INSECTS

TEXT BY **JOSIE GLAUSIUSZ**   PHOTOGRAPHS BY **VOLKER STEGER**

CHRONICLE BOOKS
SAN FRANCISCO

Library of Congress Cataloging-in-Publication
Data:
Glausiusz, Josie.
Buzz : the intimate bond between humans and
insects / text by Josie Glausiusz ; photographs by
Volker Steger.
p. cm.
ISBN 0-8118-3789-0

1. Insects—Ecology. 2. Household pests.
3. Insects as carriers of disease. I. Title.
QL496.4.G53 2004
595.717—dc22
2003016205

Book Design:
JON SUEDA & GAIL SWANLUND, *LOS ANGELES*
Typeface Design:
SWITCH—ANDREA TINNES, *BERLIN, GERMANY*
Solex—ZUZANNA LICKO, *EMIGRE*

Manufactured in China.

Distributed in Canada by Raincoast Books
9050 Shaughnessy Street
Vancouver, British Columbia V6P 6E5
10 9 8 7 6 5 4 3 2 1

Chronicle Books LLC
85 Second Street
San Francisco, California 94105
www.chroniclebooks.com

TO OUR GRANDMOTHERS,
AMELIA HARRIS AND HILDE STEGER

TABLE OF CONTENTS

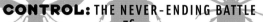

CONTROL: THE NEVER-ENDING BATTLE
76

CRIME: WELCOME TO THE BODY BANQUET
100

PETS: INSECTS AS PETS AND PERFORMERS
122

INTRODUCTION

Go to the ant, thou sluggard;
Consider her ways, and be wise:
Which having no guide, overseer or ruler
Provides her bread in the summer,
And gathers her food in the harvest.

Proverbs 6: 6–8

The origin of the word *bug* probably lies in the Middle English or Welsh word *bugge* or *bwga,* meaning scarecrow, hobgoblin or ghost. The same root has given us words like *bogey, bugbear* and *bugaboo.* Today the term *bug* is used, colloquially, to refer to both germs and to invertebrates that, in many people's minds, have sinister traits: insects, spiders, mites and others endowed with what seems like more than their fair share of legs. Perhaps no one described the common fear of bugs better than the Nobel Prize–winning poet and playwright Maurice Maeterlinck. "Something in the insect seems to be alien to the habits, morals and psychology of this world, as if it had come from some other planet, more monstrous, more energetic, more insensate, more atrocious, more infernal than our own," he wrote.

At any rate, a lot of people really loathe them. And this is strange, because of the estimated nine million species of insects on Earth—the vast majority undiscovered and unnamed—only about 1½ percent do us any harm. The rest have either no impact or provide some very obvious, often indispensable, benefits to humans. They pollinate our crops. They decompose our dead. They eat pests that destroy our own harvests, as well as many weeds. In turn they are eaten by birds, frogs, reptiles, fish and mammals, including ourselves. They have inspired artists, poets and writers with the beauty of their body ornaments, the lyricism of their songs, the diligence of their work habits. Far from being aliens, insects were inhabitants of this planet long before humans—about 400 million years longer, in fact.

Without insects, the world would look very different. All the plants that insects pollinate—including vast tracts of tropical rain forest—would disappear. By one estimate, approximately 80 percent of the world's ninety-four major crop plants are pollinated by insects, nearly all of them species of bee. Absent insects to carry sperm-containing pollen from the male parts of one flower to the ovaries of another, many plants would be unable to reproduce. Almonds, apples, blueberries, carrots, cherries, eggplants, kiwis, mangos, mustard, peaches, pepper, plums, pumpkins, sunflowers and many other fruits and vegetables would vanish or become very rare. Fig trees, fertilized only by various kinds of wasp, would go extinct.

Without insects and mites to recycle it, all the waste that we and other animals produce—from dung to discarded skin, feathers and hair—would pile up to colossal heights. Decomposition of dead bodies and plants would slow dramatically. The soil, in the absence of ants, would be less well aerated. All the animals that eat only bugs—and some unusual species of plant, such as pitcher plants and Venus flytraps—would be imperilled. Fungi and bacteria that depend upon insects for sustenance would go extinct. There would be no honey, beeswax or silk. There would also be an enormous loss of beauty. Imagine a world without butterflies, katydids, ladybugs, dragonflies or beetles burnished by every shade under the sun.

Small wonder, then, that for thousands of years insects have stirred the imagination of creative humans everywhere. Bugs show up throughout the Bible, and even the oft-despised mosquito is held up as an example by the Talmud. "Why was the mosquito created before man?" it asks. "So that if he becomes haughty he can be deflated by being told, 'the mosquito came before you.'" The ancient Egyptians held the dung-rolling scarab beetle to be sacred, depicting their sun god, Ra, as a great beetle rolling the sun, like a ball of dung, across the heavens. The study of bugs has inspired acres of prose, from the eighteenth-century scholar René-Antoine Réaumur's exhaustive seven-volume encyclopedia of insects to Vladimir Nabokov's writings on butterflies. And what would twentieth-century literature be without Franz Kafka's immortal hero Gregor Samsa, who awakes one morning from uneasy dreams to find himself transformed in his bed into a gigantic insect?

Books, art, music, movies — all have, at some point, found a muse in insects. The love of these life forms prompted artist Maria Sibylla Merian to leave her home in Amsterdam in 1699 and board a boat to Suriname, where she spent the next two years drawing its fauna before returning home loaded with brandied butterflies, boxes of pressed insects for sale and rolled vellum paintings that would later form the body of her book, *Metamorphosis of the Insects of Suriname*. Three centuries later the Belgian artist Jan Fabre would take the glittering green wing cases of nearly a million Asian jewel beetles to create a mosaic that completely covers the ceiling and chandelier of the Hall of Mirrors in the Royal Palace in Brussels. The Beatles named their band after an insect, and the composer Rimsky-Korsakov found entomological inspiration for his dazzling piece, *The Flight of the Bumble Bee*. And what would cinema be without such horror movies as *The Swarm, The Bees, The Fly* or *THEM!* the 1954 classic of monster mutant ants breeding in the deserts of New Mexico?

Yes, a small subset of bugs can injure us. They transmit disease, suck our blood, eat our stored grains. But others can heal us, live harmlessly in our houses and gardens, delight us with their odd antics, even help solve crimes. Like us, they struggle through life, seeking food, shelter, safety, the chance to mate, a place to reproduce. They dance, make music and communicate in symbols. Social insects such as ants grow subterranean crops, fight wars and even enslave one another. Instead of destroying them or their habitats, why not celebrate their many bonds with humans? Or, as the venerable Jules Michelet wrote in his 1883 epic *The Insect,* "If thou toilest and lovest, O Insect, whatever may be thy aspect, I cannot separate myself from thee. We are truly somewhat akin. For what am I myself, but a worker? What has been my greatest happiness in this world?"

HOME

STRANGERS
IN
THE BED

RIDDLE

A meal of words   made by a moth

Seemed to me   when I heard the tale

Curious   and phenomenal:

That such a mite   like a thief in the night

Should swallow up   the song of a poet,

The splendid discourse   and its solid setting!

But the strange robber   was none the wiser

For all those words   and all that eating.

(Bookworm)

Anonymous (c. 850) Translated from Anglo-Saxon
by Edwin Morgan (1976)

Lice, mice, pigeons, cockroaches

and house dust mites owe their phenomenal success in this world to one factor: They have allied themselves with humans, one of the most dominant species on the planet. Where humans go, so do rats and roaches. So too go clothes moths, bedbugs, carpet beetles, silverfish, houseflies, mosquitoes, ants and fleas—any insect that can feed on human food, human skin or human blood, or on our furnishings and fixtures, clothes, rugs and furs, on our cats, dogs, teddy bears and other fluffy toys. And of course, on the colossal quantities of garbage that we discard daily.

Human houses are the ideal home for a multitude of insects. They are warm, enclosed and filled with nooks, tunnels and pipes through which insects can scramble or hide. They are stocked with food in abundance, whether it be kitchen crumbs or book bindings or the daily shower of skin flakes that fall softly through the air, ready to be devoured by the army of dust mites that creep quietly through our beds and carpets. Few people are aware of how closely intertwined are the lives of bugs and humans. How many know that tiny mites, called demodicids, less than half a millimeter long live head-down in the roots of our eyelashes, eating oily secretions and dead skin debris, and even laying eggs in our follicles? Or that there are an estimated ten cockroaches for every human in the average major metropolis? Or that one little species of crab louse, *Phthirus pubis,* lives only among human pubic hairs, and rarely anywhere else?

But before you start screaming or scratching, ponder this: To a large extent, resistance is futile. Certainly, good personal hygiene or vigorous washing with insecticidal shampoos will help shoo away bedbugs and head lice. Frequent cleaning of kitchen cabinets might make them less enticing to ants and larder beetles. But no amount of spraying or scrubbing or squashing will ever rid our homes entirely of these arthropods.

Consider the cockroach. It is a living fossil that has endured on Earth, unchanged, for 340 million years—at least 300 million years longer than the earliest primate ancestor of humans. Cockroaches have been found in every known human habitat, from mountain caves to coal mines in England and even on the *Apollo XII* spacecraft. They have traveled to Europe on cargo boats from tropical regions of Asia, and even to the Americas on slave ships from West Africa. In their time they have weathered every sort of catastrophe, from ice ages to meteor blasts. In theory they could even withstand the level of radiation emitted by the atomic bomb dropped on Hiroshima on August 6, 1945. Experiments have shown that German cockroaches can survive a dose of radiation equaling 6,400 rads or more, approximately six times that experienced by Japanese civilians within a thirteen-mile radius of ground zero. How then could humans ever hope to annihilate them?

Why would insects ever leave us, anyway? We have made life so pleasant for them, providing every sort of comfy niche. Corks, fur coats, cigarettes and cigars, cayenne pepper, timbers, leather, parchment, even the Congressional Record have all at one time or another been infested by a variety of hardy arthropods, from moths to cigarette beetles to termites, hide beetles, bookworms and bristletails. Even the marvels of modern technology hold their own allure. Roaches, for instance, are especially drawn to the warmth and darkness of electronic equipment: fax machines, computer printers, clocks and photocopiers, as well as electrical wiring and plumbing pipes, along which they can travel about four hundred feet in a day. Cockroaches are also highly adaptive to human attack. Spray the floor, and they will migrate to the ceiling. Lay out traps and baits, and they will learn to avoid them.

Some arthropods—such as spiders—are quite helpful to have around, as they prey upon houseflies and mosquitoes. But other bugs carry diseases, and certain secretions—such as house dust mite feces as well as the saliva, cast skins and body parts of roaches—can trigger asthma and allergies. Since insect resistance has rendered many chemicals useless, humans have had to turn instead to more benign forms of insect eradication, such as removal of food and sealing of entry holes to discourage roaches from seeking residence, or fast freezing of teddy bears and rugs to rid them of carpet beetles and clothes moth larvae. These days, however, the weapon of choice is the HEPA Vac, a vacuum cleaner fitted with a "High Efficiency Particular Air" filter that can trap particles as small as .3 microns—about one four-hundredth the width of a human hair. These sucking machines can scoop up swarms of bedbugs, dust mites, clothes moths, pantry pests and carpet beetles as well as rodent droppings and dust laden with insect allergens. According to Mike Deutsch, an entomologist at the New York City–based exterminator Assured Environments, the use of these cleaners can substantially reduce the need for pesticide applications.

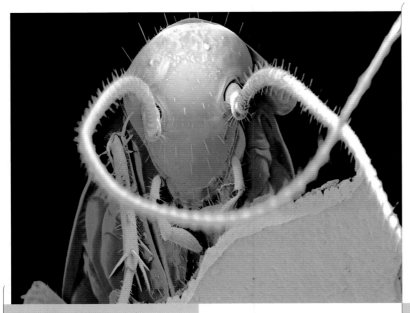

GERMAN COCKROACH
Blattella germanica

What is this creature peering curiously across the edge of an eggshell? It must be a cockroach, an insect that may rank as the most despised animal on Earth. Yet the roach has also inspired art, music, poetry, robots and reams of literature, including Franz Kafka's famous short story *Metamorphosis*, in which the unfortunate Gregor Samsa awakes one morning to find himself transformed into a gigantic insect. In fact, the roach is rather fond of literature—that is, eating it, not reading it. Glenn W. Herrick, author of *Insects Injurious to the Household and Annoying to Man* (1914) cites a traveler named Sells who gave a graphic account of the cockroach diet. It included "the bindings of books after they have been handled" as well as "leathern articles of all kinds" including saddles, harness, gloves, boots and shoes. "They crawl over and eat fruit and vegetables, dropping their egg-cases and leaving their feces and an intolerable stench wherever they travel," wrote Sells. "They also eagerly devour parchment, which material is consequently never used for wills, deeds . . . or other legal documents."

In short, the roach is not a fussy eater. This, combined with cockroaches' high fecundity, accounts for their extraordinary ubiquity. The German cockroach or *Blattella germanica*, the predominant pest roach in the world, can remain alive for three weeks without water and for six without food. No wonder they have survived virtually every attempt to eliminate them: One strain identified in the U.S. House of Representatives in 1982 was found to be resistant to nearly every available pesticide. Yet not everyone derides them. Biologist Robert Full of the University of California, Berkeley, was so impressed by the cockroach's ability to clamber nimbly over rough terrain that he helped design a six-legged robot roach called RHex that mimics the insect's springy limbs and body. The intrepid automaton can scramble over obstacles and even swim through water. Its designers hope it will one day rescue people trapped in earthquake-toppled or burning buildings.

ANT
Camponotus floridanus

"One day when I went out to my wood-pile," wrote Henry David Thoreau in his classic *Walden: or, Life in the Woods*, "I observed two large ants, the one red, the other much larger, nearly half an inch long, and black, fiercely contending with one another. Having once got hold they never let go, but struggled and wrestled and rolled on the chips incessantly." The battle to which he was witness, "the red republicans on the one hand, and the black imperialists on the other," raged with a ferocity akin to a human war, but without apparent victory on either side. Not all ant fights occur between different species, though; Florida carpenter ants, or *Camponotus floridanus*, for example, often fight over territory. If one has intruded on the other's nest, its alien smell will alert the first to the intrusion. To fend it off the defender may fight to the death, locking its mandibles on the other's antenna, or spitting acid, nipping and charging.

Living in large, tightly knit communities within nests hollowed out in wood softened by moisture or fungus, carpenter ants look after their own. Their own sisters, that is, for the ants in a single colony are all closely related, existing within a rigid hierarchy that consists of an egg-laying queen, the worker females, and the occasional male born only to mate. Those who lack the same genetic legacy cannot merit favors; hence, ants' hostile stance towards trespassers.

The opposite is true of their own queen's offspring. "No pen can describe the love, care and solicitude of the common worker ants with which they treat their young," wrote the seventeenth-century microscopist Jan Swammerdam in his treatise on insects, *The Bible of Nature*. "They neglect nothing that is necessary to feed them and bring them up." Such as sweet fluids: During the night, these reddish-brown carpenter ants can often be seen scavenging for sugary juice around soda machines. Their nests are common in attics and closets and fuse boxes, and, in one extreme case, a pay phone. For easy access they follow trails along the wires leading into homes, or use branches as bridges to safe spots under the roof.

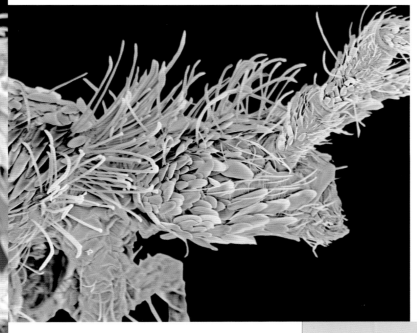

SPRINGTAILS
Collembola

Found in a flowerpot, these two sparring springtails are examples of the oldest and most primitive insects on Earth. Classified in the insect order Collembola, from a Greek word meaning "gluey peg" these wingless arthropods have been in existence for at least 400 million years; their oldest fossil ancestor was discovered in the Devonian shales of Scotland. Springtails are also among the most abundant of insects. According to Vincent B. Wigglesworth in his book *The Life of Insects*, one acre of English meadow can be home to nearly 250 million of these six-legged leapers.

Springtails could win the long jump at the insect Olympics. Attached to their abdomen is a forked organ called a furcula, which is held in a cocked position by a special catch, the tenaculum. When the tenaculum is released, the furcula snaps down and propels the animals up to twenty centimeters through the air—a distance fifty to one hundred times their own body length—enabling them to spring away from predators. The gluey peg, or collophore, is another unique organ. Once considered an adhesive appendage, it is now thought to absorb water from the environment. Springtails are fond of the damp, living in leaf litter or decaying wood, creeping into basements and drains, and scavenging on fungi, decaying plants, molds or algae.

Some six thousand species of Collembola live on the planet, occupying every niche from tropical rain forests to Antarctica and the Australian outback. Considering their scatter-shot method of sexual reproduction, their success is astounding. Males simply plant a small packet of sperm on the tip of a stalk in the soil, like a little mushroom. When a female rubs her rear end against it, the packet breaks open and the sperm swim into her vagina.

WOOD LOUSE
Porcellio scaber

Once, in sixteenth-century England, a singular honor was conferred upon the humble wood louse. In a series of stained-glass windows illustrating the signs of the zodiac in St. Mary's Church, Shrewsbury, an image of a wood louse was depicted with the Latin words *sol in cancro* (Sun in Cancer) written over its little arched back. Never mind that the artist had apparently confused it with a crab; its creator wasn't far wrong. This half-inch-long wood louse is neither true louse nor even an insect: it is a crustacean, a relative of shrimp, crabs and lobsters, and one of the few such creatures to have invaded land. Its watery origins are still evident, though, for the fourteen-legged wood louse—also known as the sow bug, tiggy-hog or parsons-pig—favors dark, humid haunts: compost heaps, flowerpots, decaying vegetation. Lacking the waxy cuticle that covers the insect exoskeleton, wood lice have adapted to the threat of water loss in other ways. They huddle together in packs to reduce evaporation and siphon water from droplets with the aid of anal appendages called uropods.

Porcellio scaber, pictured here, is not a pest. Far from it. As consumers and recyclers of decaying matter, wood lice play an important role in returning nutrients to the soil. One relative of the wood louse, the roly-poly pill bug or *Armadillidium vulgare*, was once observed en masse devouring an entire dead rat. These little scuttlers can also serve another useful function. Because their blood pigment, hemocyanin, is copper-based, they scavenge this metal, as well as cadmium, copper, lead and zinc, from the soil. Thus the presence of these heavy metals in their tissues is a very good guide to local toxic waste–contaminated ground. Since they are found almost everywhere on Earth—introduced by humans even to remote oceanic islands—one zoologist, Steve Hopkin of the University of Reading in the U.K., has proposed setting up a "wood louse watch" scheme using these crustaceans as mini-monitors of global environmental pollution.

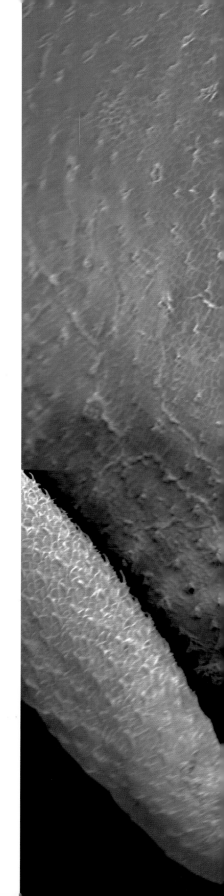

SILVERFISH
Lepisma saccharina

The silverfish is a shy sort of insect, nervous of bright lights and keen to escape the hand of an oncoming human. "It appears to the naked eye as a glistening Pearl-colored Moth," wrote the great seventeenth-century experimental scientist Robert Hooke, "which upon the removing of Books and Papers in the Summer is observed nimbly to scud and pack away to some lurking cranney where it may the better protect itself from appearing dangers."

One of the most primitive insects known, the silverfish is a wingless creature that can nevertheless run extremely rapidly if uncovered from one of the many dark crevices in which it hides: under rocks and trees, or nestled inside bookcases, attics, basements or behind the wallpaper. Librarians loathe them. That's because *Lepisma saccharina*, the "sugar guest," is particularly partial to any food rich in carbohydrates: flour, paper, the glue found in bookbindings, starched collars and cuffs, gum, lace, rayon, cotton and linen. And also, on occasion, the molted skins and dead bodies of its fellow "fish." The damage they inflict upon books is especially insidious: using their jawlike mandibles, they graze upon paper, leaving behind little notches and holes and sometimes loose feces and yellow stains, and even the shimmering silver scales that cover their abdomens.

The silverfish brings new meaning to the notion of the doubtful guest, the unwelcome visitor that slips in and stays for years, quietly chomping away at the household supplies. Silverfish can live for three years or longer, laying up to one hundred eggs over their lifespan, which they secrete in crevices or cracks. Not all species favor human houses. One enterprising gate-crasher, the ant silverfish, lives uninvited in ant nests, stealing drops of honey straight out of the jaws of its unwitting hosts.

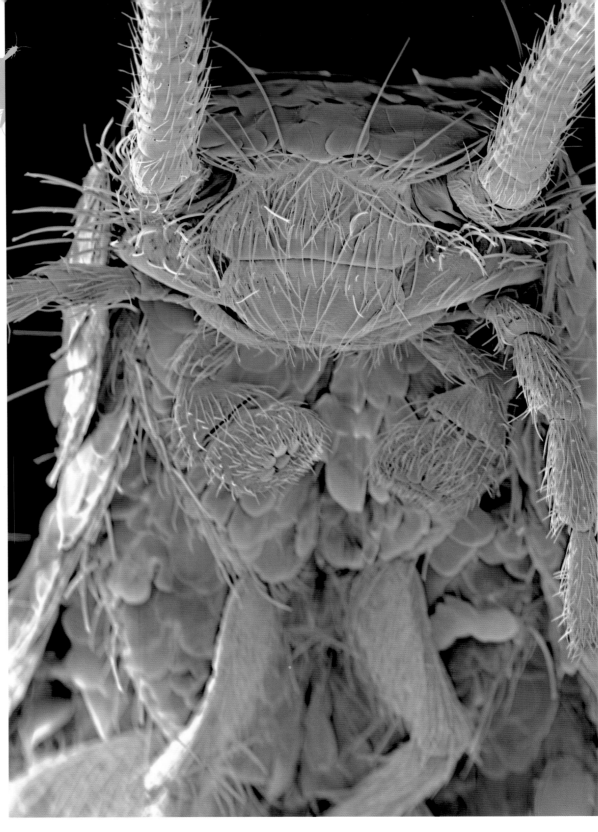

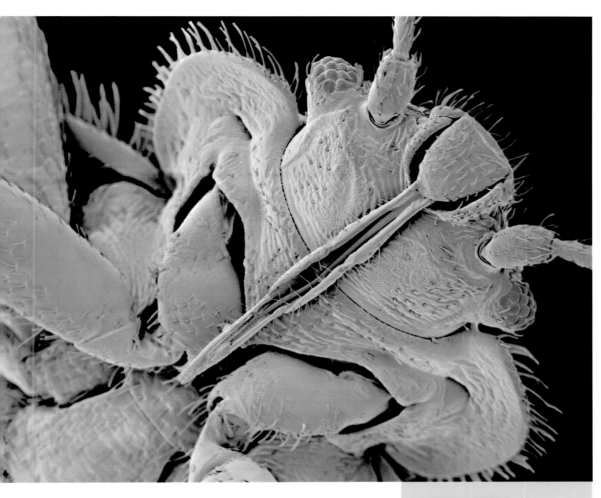

COMMON BEDBUG
Cimex lectularius

This bug is a strange bedfellow, and for much of human history it has been hard to dislodge. "It is said to have its origin in warm blood, and has an extravagant fondness for humans," wrote the fourteenth-century Egyptian Kamal al-Din al-Damiri of the bedbug in his *Dictionary of the Life of Animals*, an illustrated compendium of beastly lore. Al-Damiri may have been mistaken about the first piece of information, but he was accurate about the second:

Cimex lectularius seems to have been our companion since we first took to dwelling in caves.

At least twelve species of bloodsucking *Cimex* bugs are parasites of bats, and many others feed on cave-nesting birds. This one probably followed humans to all manner of shelters and homes, hiding by day in the walls of houses, or inside bedding or cracks in bed frames, emerging by night to quaff the blood the bug needs to molt from nymph to adult. Though it does not transmit disease, it is extremely annoying, as its saliva triggers large itchy bumps on the skin; and excessive biting can cause anemia in infants.

Male bedbugs have been called "the sex maniacs of the insect world" since there seems to be no limit to their lust: They will mate with females repeatedly, both of their own and other species, and with other males as well. The act as performed by the bedbug, called traumatic insemination, is also highly unusual—the male takes his copulatory organ, called a paramere, and stabs the female in the abdomen; from there, the sperm must migrate internally to her oviducts. Strange sex acts in bed may be the least that humans have to fear, though. Once driven away by DDT, bedbugs and their biting ways appear to be making a comeback, fueled by international travel and the trade in old furniture at flea-markets. Perhaps to compensate for their ubiquity, the ancients attributed to them medicinal powers; the Roman Pliny the Elder, for example, recommended them for snakebites. "Seven bed bugs mingled with water were a dose for a man, while four were sufficient for children," writes Glenn Herrick in *Insects Injurious to the Household and Annoying to Man*. "The smell of them will [also] relieve 'hysterical suffocation.'"

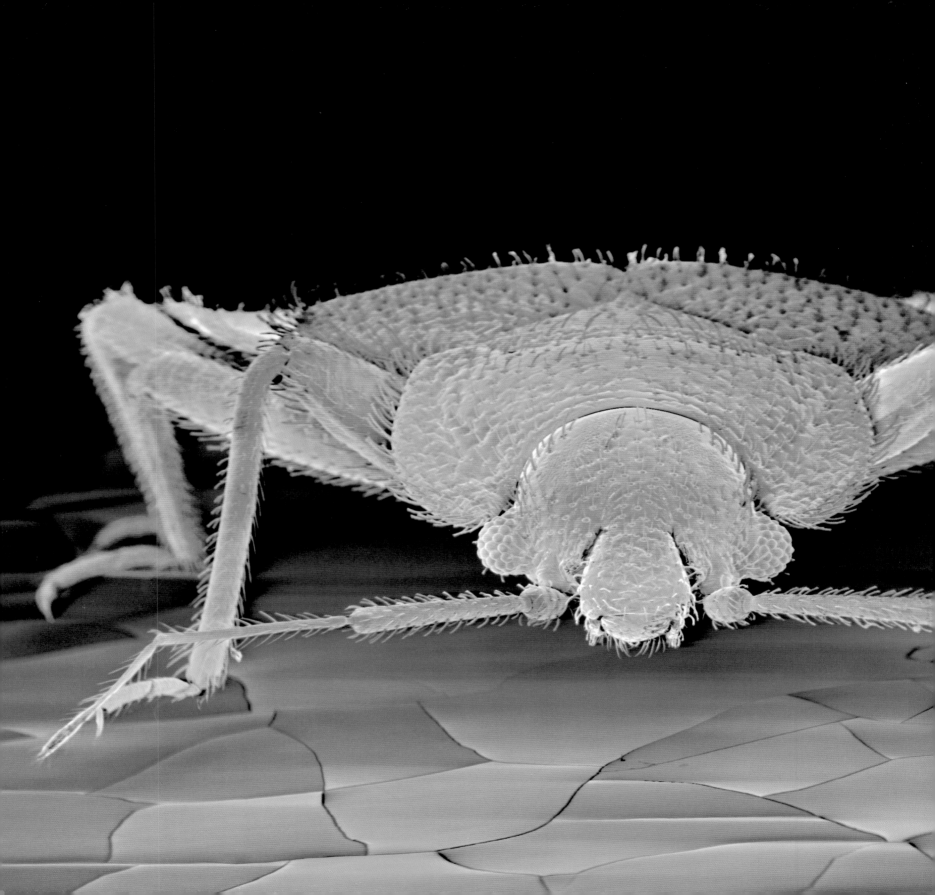

COMMON BEDBUG
Cimex lectularius

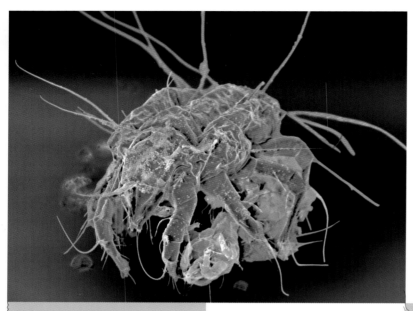

HOUSE DUST MITE
Dermatophagoides pteronyssinus

Say hello to the skin eaters. Yes, skin flakes are the favorite food of these two house dust mites. Near-invisible to the naked eye, but near-cosmopolitan in its living habits, the house dust mite, *Dermatophagoides pteronyssinus,* may be our most common companion. One typical bed may contain anywhere between ten thousand to ten million mites, all blindly chewing away on our discarded skin, and depositing little fecal pellets on our sheets and pillows. In fact, it's been estimated that 10 percent of the weight of a two-year-old pillow is composed of dead mites and their droppings —dung that the dust mite may reingest as many as three times. Wrapped in a special film, the droppings incorporate powerful mite enzymes that continue to digest food particles even after they have left this skin grazer's gut.

Dust mites are a boon and a bane to humans. In a way, they provide household help by hoovering up the mountains of skin we each shed—by one estimate, as much as five to ten grams in a week. How soon would we be enveloped in acres of superfluous skin flakes were it not for their presence? Not everyone appreciates such domestic aid, though. Those who are allergic to factors in their feces, particularly a potent protein-digesting enzyme called *Der p 1* that is produced in the mite's digestive juices, would sooner be rid of these eight-legged vacuum cleaners. A powerful promoter of asthma and hay fever, *Der p 1* is so invasive that it has even been found in fetal amniotic fluid and in the cord blood of some newborn babies.

Ridding the home of dust mites isn't easy, however, because they nest nearly everywhere, from sofas to soft toys to carpets and even on the scalp, where they dine on dandruff. The one thing dust mites never do is drink; instead they suck moisture from the air, so dry conditions will kill them or drive them away. In fact, male dust mites are so sensitive to dehydration that they will huddle together to increase the humidity. Targeting the chemicals that trigger such clusters may be one way to control this ubiquitous creature.

CLOTHES MOTH
Tineola bisselliella

Warning: Your sweaters may be seething with life. Do you think they are sitting calmly in the closet, silently awaiting the end of summer? Maybe they are; or maybe they are being chewed ragged by the offspring of the clothes moth, *Tineola bisselliella*. This one is an adult, so it hasn't taken a bite since it emerged from its silken cocoon. It lives only to reproduce, but its grubs are very greedy. Clothes moth larvae, sequestered in dark wardrobes and cabinets, feed on wool, feathers, leather, fur and many other fabrics left undisturbed for long periods in antique dolls and teddy bears, hats and upholstery, bristle brushes, wall hangings, wool carpets and even the felt on piano hammers. These creamy-colored crawlers are blessed—or cursed, depending on your point of view—with an enzyme that can digest keratin, a tough protein found in hair, fur, hooves and nails. But they also obtain nutrients elsewhere, such as B vitamins and minerals found in fabric stains caused by urine, hair oil, sweat, fruit juice, milk and beer.

How to combat a clothes moth infestation? Well, you could try the remedy recommended by preacher Johann Colerus in his *Household Book*, published in about 1590. "If wormwood or aniseed or goat's liver, two or three cedar twigs, the rind of a lemon or citrus fruit or pieces of fern are placed in cupboards with clothes or between clothes, they will drive out moths and cockroaches," he wrote. Should goat liver be hard to obtain, then moth balls may be the answer, unless you have curious children rummaging around in your wardrobe. Moth balls are also toxic to humans, but pheromone traps, exuding a heady mix of sex attractants, entice only male moths to a sticky death. The best way to keep closets moth-free, though, is to deny them entry in the first place. Because the larvae like to snuggle deep in dim undisturbed nooks, simply cleaning and airing clothes and carpets may be sufficient to shake them loose. If all else fails, pop that old stuffed bear in the freezer for a fortnight.

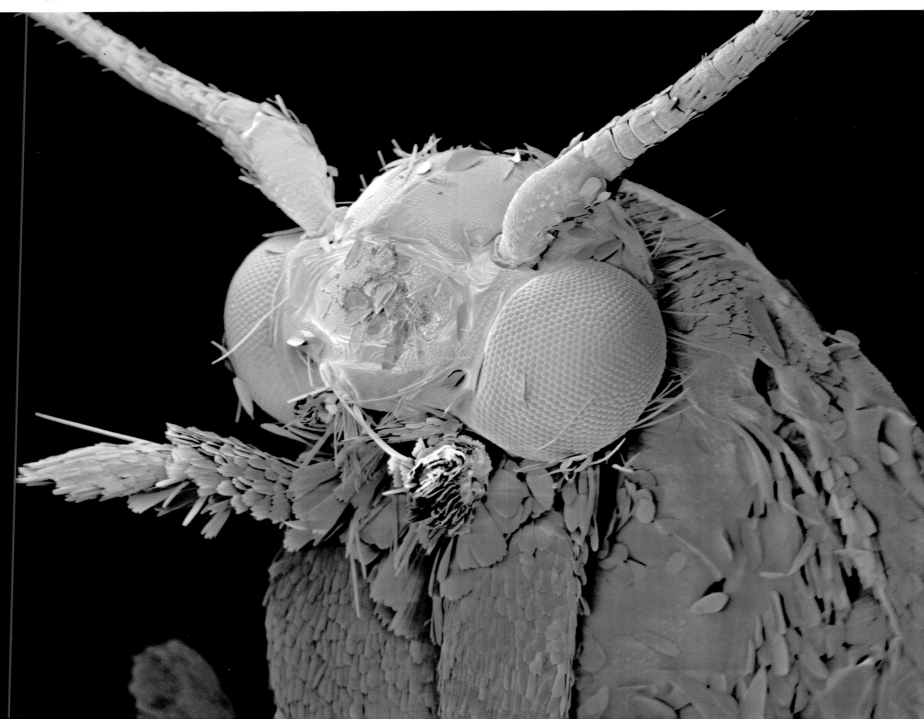

WARDROBE BEETLE
Attagenus fasciatus

If only this bug had stayed where it evolved, museums would pay it no mind. The natural habitat of this larva of the wardrobe beetle, *Attagenus fasciatus,* is a bird or mammal nest, where it eats and recycles fur, skin, feathers and excreta. "In the natural order of things, they are very useful. If we didn't have them we'd be three feet deep in dead birds," says British entomologist David Pinniger, an expert on museum infestations. Sadly, these bugs don't stop at dead bird detritus. Their larvae and those of related carpet beetles often invade textile collections, attacking almost anything containing the fibrous protein keratin: wool, rawhide, vellum, stained silk, dolls with human hair, military uniforms, teddy bears, even other insects. Sometimes known as "woolly bears," these short, fat, hairy beetle larvae are wanderers: they will chew a hole in one spot, pause, crawl a few feet, gnaw at another site, stop, creep and start munching anew.

What havoc they can wreak. In one case Pinniger cites, a museum case full of butterflies was almost entirely eaten by carpet beetle larvae, who left behind only the pins and labels—and a pile of discarded wings, apparently deemed less tasty than the butterflies' fat-filled bodies. Pinniger has also seen antique royal garments ruined, and even a pockmarked coat that once belonged to Lord Nelson. Quite the most bizarre attack occurred at a branch of London's Natural History Museum. As if to add insult to injury, a stuffed quagga—a subspecies of zebra hunted to extinction in South Africa over one hundred years ago—was ravaged once again after falling prey not to shotgun-toting settlers but to carpet beetle larvae. "Somebody noticed large lumps of hair falling out of it," recalls Pinniger. "When we looked at it, it was being eaten by woolly bears. Of course, you can't go and get another quagga; it's extinct. It was completely irreplaceable."

BLACK CARPET BEETLE
Attagenus unicolor

The great British naturalist J. B. S. Haldane was once asked what one could infer about the work of God from a study of his works. "He has an inordinate fondness for beetles," he was said to have replied. With approximately 350,000 species on the planet, occupying every niche from ice cap rims to cat food, the beetle is one huge success story. Some species are seen as sacred, like the Egyptian scarab or the New Zealand giraffe beetle, the Maori god of the new-made canoe; many others are celebrated for their beauty and even transformed into works of art. This one, the larva of the black carpet beetle, prefers to transform works of art into tatters. Tapestries, oriental rugs, textiles: it's all fair game for the larva of *Attagenus unicolor*, a carrot-shaped wriggler with a tuft of long hairs at its tail.

Black carpet beetle larvae can live for two to three years in dark crevices indoors, but the adults are free-flying forms attracted to sunlight. In early summer they can be found feeding on the pollen of spiraea and crape myrtle flowers. In Europe, warmer weather linked to global climate change is thought to have contributed to the spread of two related species. The Guernsey carpet beetle, originally identified in a house on the island in 1961, was found in a London museum two years later and has since migrated northward to Scotland. The brown carpet beetle or *Attagenus smirnovi*—whimsically dubbed the "vodka beetle"—originated in Moscow and is now a major domestic pest in Denmark. Warmer climes speed generation times: the varied carpet beetle in Britain now takes one year instead of two to complete its entire life cycle. Yet carpet beetles are also tolerant of cold, so to kill them pest controllers must freeze them at a temperature of minus eighteen Celsius or lower. Suffocating them in pure nitrogen gas—thus starving them of oxygen—is also good for booting the beetles out of their nooks.

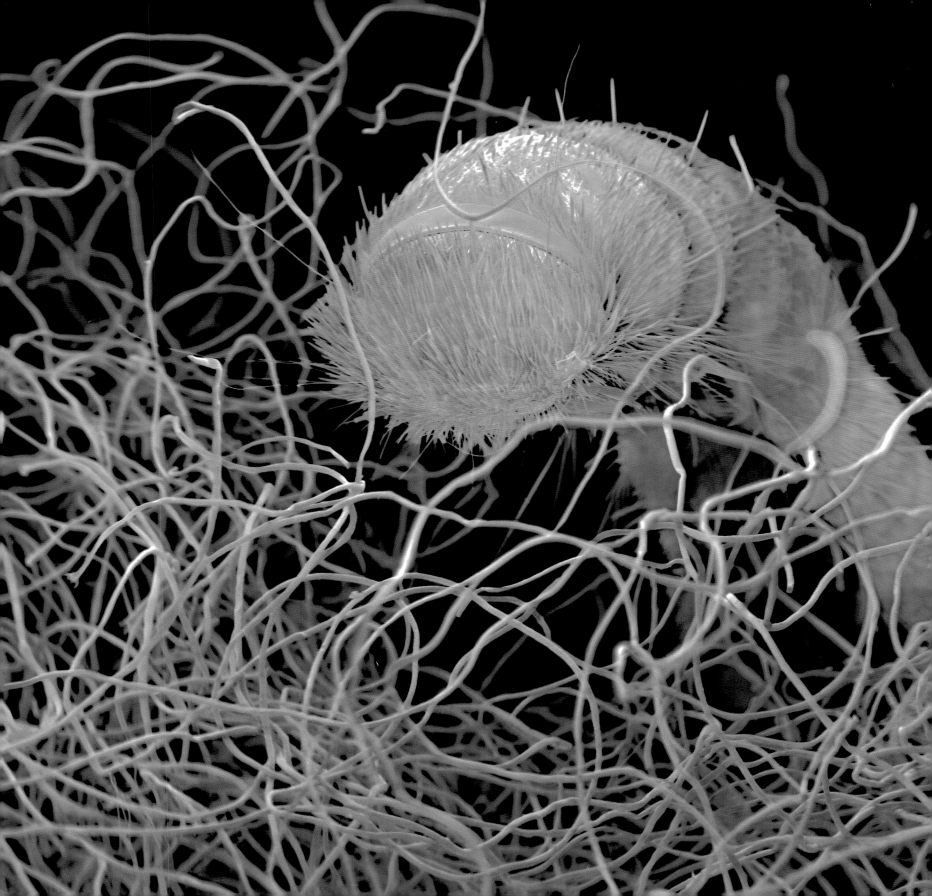

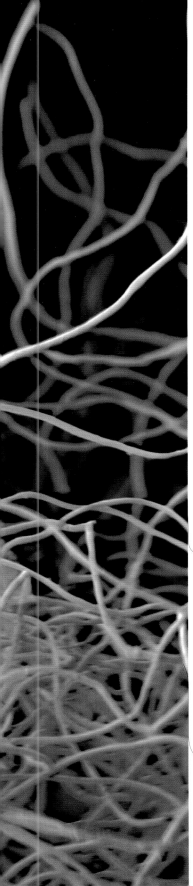

BLACK CARPET BEETLE
Attagenus unicolor

RUB-A-DUB-DUB, THANKS FOR THE GRUB

Whoever sows will have empty bins

However, a better field;

Whoever keeps the bin full

Will be damaged by granary insects, rats and disaster!

Rumi, 1207–1273 C.E., *Problem of Stinginess*

Put cream and sugar on a fly, and it tastes very much like a black raspberry.

E. W. Howe, *Country Town Sayings*

Why Not Eat Insects?

is the title of a short polemic published in 1885 by Vincent Holt. In it he argues that insects are nutritious, delicious and readily available; the only obstacle to their widespread consumption, it would seem, is the inbred disgust many people feel at swallowing, say, sautéed silkworms or curried cockchafers. Dress them up with a few fancy French names, though, and those who spurn insect cuisine might just be tempted. After all, escargots are frequently offered in many respected restaurants. So why not *Choufleurs garnies de Chenilles* (cauliflowers garnished with caterpillars) as Holt suggests in a sample menu? Or *Cerfs Volant à la Gru Gru* (stag beetle larvae on toast)? For dessert, perchance, a dish of *Crème de Groseilles aux Nemates* (gooseberry cream with sawflies)?

Holt did not, in fact, address his book to the discerning French gourmet. His audience, or so he saw it, was the poor, who—fools that they were—would rather complain of starvation than gather grubs and grill them. "In the country the poorer labourers and their families go on week after week, attempting to keep body and soul together with nothing but bread," wrote Holt. "Yes, meat is dear; but the wheat crop would have been twice as thick if the wireworms, the leatherjackets, and the luscious white chafer grubs had been diligently collected by you for food. Meal-worms are fattening. You should have hand-picked your cabbages and gooseberry trees, so that you might enjoy and profit by their would-be destroyers."

What explained the popular aversion to insectivory? "Ridiculous fastidiousness," replied Holt's contemporary Jules Michelet in his own treatise, *The Insect*, "has debarred our Western peoples from one of the richest and most exquisite sources of nourishment."

Yet in much of the rest of the world, entomophagy, or bug eating, is not only common but relished. Wander the markets of Oaxaca in Mexico, and one can see spicy pan-fried grasshoppers for sale by the trayload. Elsewhere in Mexico, *escamoles*, or black ant larvae, are served up with diced onion and shreds of cilantro, as well as *moscos de pajaro*, the eggs of water bugs, which are ground up and toasted into little cakes. In Australia, indigenous peoples are reported to feast upon bogong moths, gathered in the mountain caves of New South Wales, and witchety grubs, acacia-root-feeding caterpillars of the large Cossid moth. In Thailand, salted silkworm pupae are considered a delicacy, as are mangdana, or giant water bugs, which

are often tossed into a salad. Most popular of all may be locusts, commonly eaten in the Middle East and Africa after being gutted and roasted whole, or ground into flour or boiled in saltwater and dried in the sun.

The locust-eating habit goes back, in fact, to the earliest times. The biblical Book of Leviticus, which forbids the consumption of pigs, bats, rats, owls, geckos and chameleons, does permit the eating of selected "flying creeping things": *The locust after its kind, and the grasshopper after its kind, and the hargol after its kind, and the hagav after its kind*, the latter two being different forms of migratory and solitary locusts. The Gospel of Matthew reports that John the Baptist's diet consisted of locusts and wild honey. The Koran also mentions meals made of locusts, and the wives of the prophet Mohammed were said to both accept them and send them out as gifts.

What is more sensible, after all, than eating the pest that devours your crops? If gigantic swarms of locusts descend upon your fields and eat every green sprout, what is left to eat but the insects themselves? Insects that are remarkably nutritious. According to data compiled by Iowa State University, one hundred grams of small grasshoppers contain about twenty grams of protein and only six grams of fat, as compared to twenty-four grams of protein and eighteen grams of fat in lean ground beef. The grasshoppers also have about four times as much calcium and more than twice as much iron as beef. Caterpillars contain many times more thiamine, riboflavin and niacin as beef or cod. Eating insects also appears to be more ecologically sound than beef or lamb consumption. To raise cattle and sheep requires large tracts of land and huge amounts of feed, producing, respectively, only ten and five pounds of meat for every hundred pounds of feed they are fed.

The truth is, though, that we all eat insects all the time, whether we admit it or not. Whether nestled in between the broccoli fronds or concealed inside corn kernels, insects enter our diet clandestinely and always have. The U.S. Food and Drug Administration recognizes this and, rather than order manufacturers to eliminate all traces of insects from every food, sets limits on acceptable levels of bugs. Frozen Brussels sprouts, for example, are allowed an average of thirty or more aphids per one hundred grams before action need be taken. Canned sweet corn must be discarded only if the aggregate length of corn ear worms or corn borer larvae or their cast skins exceeds twelve millimeters in twenty-four pounds of kernels. Pitted dates are condemned only if 5 percent or more of each batch are contaminated by dead insects or their excreta. And golden raisins are permitted up to thirty-five fruit fly eggs per eight ounces of fruit.

The list is very long, and with good reason: Insects are as fond of our food as we are and will find a way into even the most cleverly constructed silo or storehouse. But be consoled, your food may be flavored with bugs, but the added nutrients are completely free.

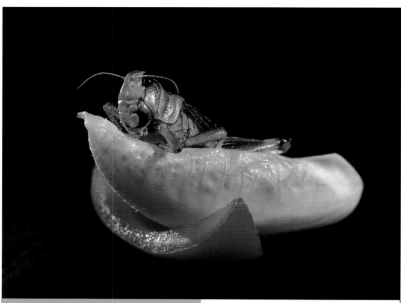

AFRICAN MIGRATORY LOCUST
Locusta migratoria

Jean-Henri Fabre, the nineteenth-century naturalist known as the "entomological philosopher," once described an unusual meal he served up to a selection of guests. "I capture some fat Locusts and have them cooked in a very rough and ready fashion, fried with butter and salt," he wrote in his book *The Life of the Grasshopper*. "We all of us, big and little, partake of the queer dish at dinner [. . .] It has a certain shrimpy flavor, a taste that reminds one of grilled Crab; and, were it not that the shell is very tough for such slight edible contents, I would go to the length of saying that it is good, without, however, feeling any desire for more."

Fabre, who dedicated his entire life to the study of insects, was not the first philosopher to dabble in entomophagy; Aristotle, who was partial to a plate of cicadas, pronounced the nymphs the tastiest, or, after copulation, "the females, which are then full of white eggs." Nowadays, epicures in search of such curious cuisine can experiment in the privacy of their own home, with the aid of such manuals as

David George Gordon's delightfully disgusting *Eat-A-Bug Cookbook*. Or they can pay a visit to Soda, the Berlin eatery whose menu is replete with insect entrées and desserts—such as this migratory locust, which has ended its travels atop a leaf of chicory. Frank Ochmann, the chef who cooks these crunchy treats, first freezes the insects in order to kill them, then plucks off their wings and their spiky rear legs, which can catch in customers' throats. Then he roasts the locusts. Or he fries them with herbs and garlic and serves them with couscous and curry, as a garnish on a salad, or stirred into a dish of noodles. Appreciative diners—of whom there are, apparently, no shortage—describe the insects' flavor as reminiscent of roasted chestnuts.

CHOCOLATE-COVERED
Locusta migratoria

What an ignominious end for this migratory locust—toasted and coated in chocolate and served on a peach slice with a sliver of strawberry. In another life it could have been part of a magnificent swarm, stretching for several hundred square miles and flying fantastic distances across Africa, the Mediterranean, and eastern Asia, eating its weight in green vegetation each day. The sort described by Pliny, "which fly with such noise of wings that they are believed to be birds, and they obscure the sun, making the nations gaze upward in anxiety lest they should settle all over their lands."

A chocolate crust does, however, have one big advantage: it disguises the fact that the food one is about to eat is of arthropod origin. "The first time people see it, they think, woo, never!" says chef Frank Ochmann of Soda in Berlin, who prepared this particular bonbon. "But when you begin with the chocolate, you taste only the chocolate and something in the middle that's a little bit crunchy, like a nut. Then you think, ja, it's OK, good, again, one more."

Strange but true: Many people who would happily dine on bottom-dwelling lobsters and sea scavengers like shrimp would recoil in horror at the thought of eating an insect. Perhaps it is because they associate bugs with dirt and disease. In fact, raw bugs *can* carry parasitic worms that can be passed on to people. If thoroughly boiled or baked, though, they are perfectly healthy. For choice cuts choose the legs and tail, which consist of large filaments of longitudinal muscle; but be careful of the exoskeleton, which is not particularly palatable. It is comprised of chitin, a tough carbohydrate that gives strength to this outer structure. It is also indigestible, and, as experienced insect eaters are aware, it has an awkward tendency to lodge itself, in shards, between the chewer's teeth.

YELLOW MEALWORM LARVA
Tenebrio molitor
AND SUPERWORM LARVA
Zophobas morio

Revenge is sweet. Or in this case, sautéed. Impaled on the tines of this fork are two pests of stored grain: *Tenebrio molitor*, the small yellow mealworm larvae, and *Zophobas morio,* the fat, succulent super-worms. What better way to dispatch your enemies than to eat them?

As it happens, there is no shortage of recipes for serving these squirming hors d'oeuvres. One can pop them inside a slice of leek and offer them up with a sprig of rosemary. One can chop them up and stir-fry them with bean sprouts, water chest-nuts, green peppers, onions, eggs and soy sauce, as Ronald Taylor and Barbara Carter suggest in a recipe for egg foo yung that appears in their book *Entertaining with Insects, Or: The Original Guide to Insect Cookery*. Turn them into cookies by baking dry crumbled mealworms with flour, brown sugar, vanilla, eggs, butter and chocolate chips. For the spiritually inclined, there are David George Gordon's strictly non-kosher Larval Latkes, wormy pancakes topped with sour cream and applesauce and served in honor of the Jewish festival of Chanukah.

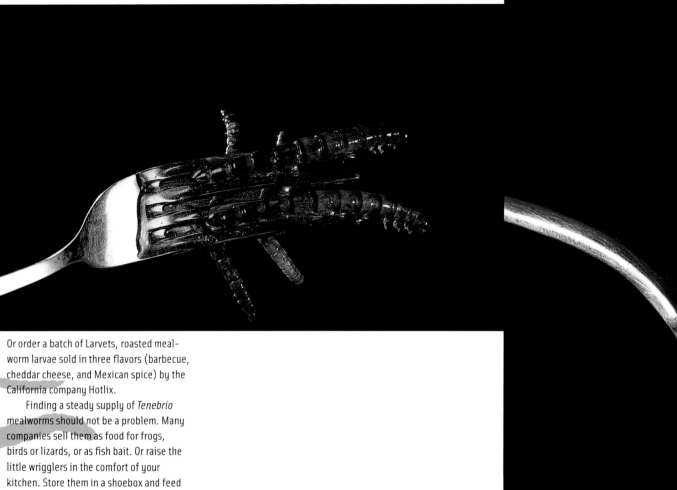

Or order a batch of Larvets, roasted meal-worm larvae sold in three flavors (barbecue, cheddar cheese, and Mexican spice) by the California company Hotlix.

Finding a steady supply of *Tenebrio* mealworms should not be a problem. Many companies sell them as food for frogs, birds or lizards, or as fish bait. Or raise the little wrigglers in the comfort of your kitchen. Store them in a shoebox and feed them every four to five days with oatmeal or wheat bran, adding a slice of apple or carrot for moisture. To stop them from turning into adult beetles, simply place them in the refrigerator, where the cold will inhibit their growth.

HOUSE CRICKET
Acheta domesticus

Peter Lund Simmonds, in his Victorian classic *Curiosities of Food: Or the Dainties and Delicacies of Different Nations Obtained from the Animal Kingdom*, once suggested that the Latin name for the field cricket, *Gryllus*, was an open invitation to do just that. One wonders how seriously one ought to take him, considering he also included recipes in his book for Baked Elephants' Paws, Flamingoes' Tongues and Fried Rattlesnake. Still, there's no doubt that crickets have been an important source of protein in some cultures for long periods of time. Native Americans in northern Nevada, for example, were said to hunt Mormon crickets by digging thirty-foot-long trenches covered in stiff grass. After driving them into the pits with the aid of swinging fans, they set fire to the grass and roasted the crickets for dinner.

This cricket perched on a piece of tomato is not a field cricket but its slender and delicate yellow-brown cousin the European house cricket, *Acheta domesticus*.

A heat-loving creature, it lives in basements and bakeries, or on warm spots outdoors, like garbage dumps. "House Crickets with their chirping and calling are a troublesome thing in the house for a landlord, since they often fall into the food and drink of men and animals," wrote Johann Colerus in his 1590 *Household Book*. Sometimes the fall is deliberate, as when enterprising cooks allow them to drop into the orzo, or sprinkle them on top of a chocolate torte. Their flavor is of mild shrimp, though even that is often disguised by the condiments in which they are cooked.

It is of course the cricket's "chirping and calling" for which it is celebrated, not its crunchy texture. Crickets call by rubbing one forewing against the other, drawing a file on one wing like a violin bow across a scraper on the other. The male song is so powerful that females can be drawn to it from great distances. Just before World War I, a German scientist showed that female crickets will jump to a telephone if a male of the same species is crooning at the other end of the line.

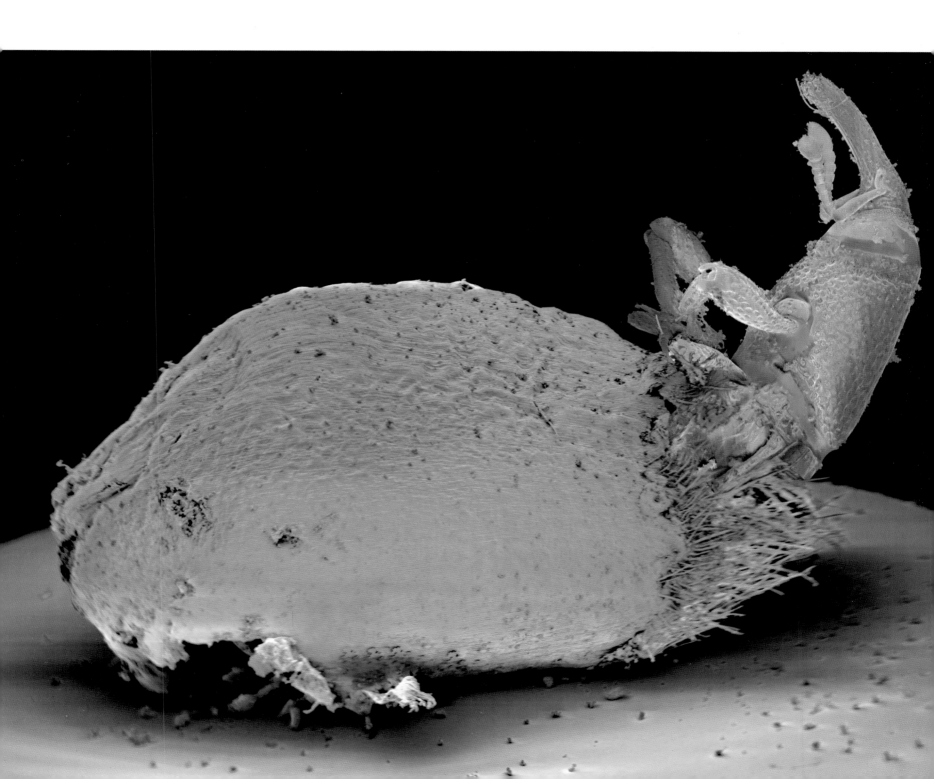

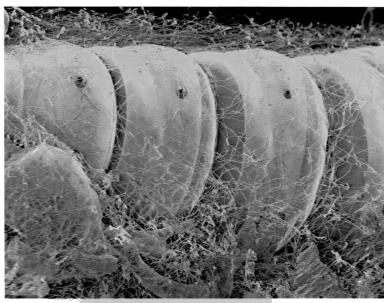

GRANARY WEEVIL
Sitophilus granarius

Let them gather all the food of those good years that come, and lay up corn under the hand of Pharoah, writes the biblical Book of Genesis. *And that food shall be for store to the land against the seven years of famine, which shall be in the land of Egypt.* The instruction bears testimony to the Egyptian invention of grain storage some 4,500 years ago. Alas, along with grain storage came granary weevils, specifically the long-snouted *Sitophilus granarius*, shown here escaping from a grain of wheat. That the granary weevil was a pest to the Egyptians is without doubt: a specimen of the insect was found in 1950 in the 4,585-year-old tomb of Queen Ichetis in the step pyramid at Saqqara.

Once an acorn eater, *Sitophilus* is now one of the most destructive grain insects in the world, sometimes devouring the entire contents of farmers' bins or cargo ships. Polished-black wingless females chew cavities in kernels of corn, wheat, oats, barley and buckwheat, laying an egg in each one, and sealing such holes, up to four hundred in all, with a gelatinous secretion. There the eggs hatch within days into soft white plump and legless grubs, which proceed to hollow out the grain before pupating and emerging as adults, and leaving behind a mass of frass and hulls.

Because most of its life cycle occurs concealed inside kernels, control of the granary weevil can be difficult. Cooling the grain to a temperature of minus-seven degrees Celsius for six weeks can be quite effective, as can fumigation. One potential biological control agent is the Anisopteromalus wasp, which seeks out infested seeds and lays its eggs not in the kernel but in the weevil grub, whose body fluids are then consumed by the wasp larva. The ancient Egyptians, however, had their own control methods. They smeared rancid cat and bird fat, as well as gazelle dung, on the walls of their dome-shaped storage chambers.

WAREHOUSE MOTH
Ephestia elutella

Stored grain is a sort of desert—food-rich, but bone dry and thinly populated. But even a desert has its denizens, its nomads and its camels. It just so happens that this warehouse moth larva, *Ephestia elutella*, is not only a willing inhabitant of all forms of stored cereals, rice, nuts, herbal teas, spices and cocoa, but is also able to make the desert bloom. These larvae take the carbohydrate in grain and turn it into energy, carbon dioxide and water. The moisture attracts mites and others insects, which respire in turn, releasing more water and raising the temperature. The warmth and the damp promote the growth of toxic fungi and bacteria, producing a fermenting quagmire that no human would care to sample. Sometimes the whole mess can even ignite when microbe-secreted methane, a flammable gas, catches fire inside a grain silo.

One grain of dry wheat is only 12 to 14 percent water, and it is tough to chew. *Ephestia* larvae, however, are superbly well-adapted to infest it. They have strong mouthparts with which to gnaw the grain and a lipid layer coating their cuticle that reduces the loss of water. They conceal themselves beneath a mesh of webbing, which protects them from spiders and parasitic wasps. Adult *Ephestia* moths also have a fine sense of smell, finding stored grain from afar, and they are not deterred by insect screens; they simply lay their eggs on its surface, and the larvae that hatch out crawl through the holes. They are so tiny—just one-tenth of a millimeter in diameter—that they can even slink along the channel in a loosely sealed screw-top jar.

Ephestia is a very ancient pest. Its name is derived from the Greek word *epihestos*, meaning "on top of the kitchen." "There are worms in dried figs and dates," says the Talmud. "The date worm does not live twelve months, like all boneless animals, and it must therefore have entered the date after the harvest."

INDIAN MEAL MOTH
Plodia interpunctella

That big boulder on which this bug is roosting is a raisin. This Indian meal moth just *loves* muesli. It also adores chocolate, especially the nut-studded sort. Dried fruit? Yes please. Herbal teas? Much obliged. Candy? Old cookies? Powdered milk? Bee excrement? *Dee-lish. Plodia interpunctella* is a cosmopolitan sort of food pest, common in kitchens and grocery stores (as well as in beehives) but not keen on company. If one *Plodia* larva meets another coming through the rye (or the corn or the cocoa) each will exude a brown liquid from its mouth, which acts as a repellant. Sadly for *Plodia*, it also acts as an attractant—to a parasitic wasp called *Venturia canescens*. If the wasp finds a larva it will lay an egg inside it, making the wasp an appealing agent of biological control.

Benign methods of controlling the caterpillar are important because chemical fumigants can be toxic and not always effective. Methyl bromide, a once-common chemical, is being phased out under the 1987 Montreal Protocol on Substances that Deplete the Ozone Layer. Heating warehouses to high temperatures is an option, but only if they are empty—and then every nook and cranny must be thoroughly baked. Meanwhile, studies show that both *Venturia* and another wasp, *Habrobracon hebetor*, which stings and paralyzes host larvae before laying eggs in them, can effectively reduce populations of *Plodia* if introduced into storage facilities in autumn.

What if an infestation is suspected but cannot be seen? In that case, exterminators use a crafty trick to detect possible pests: They lower a long microphone into the grain and listen for nibbling. "The sound is a little bit like the crunching when you eat cornflakes, or like pebbles in a river, little clicking sounds," says Cornel Adler, a biologist at in Germany's Federal Biological Research Center. "If you attach this microphone to a computer, you could develop something that distinguishes species and the different larval stages."

CIGARETTE BEETLE
Lasioderma serricorne

All the health warnings in the world would not deter this beetle from its favorite weed: tobacco. The cigarette beetle, *Lasioderma serricorne*, is one of the most destructive pests of stored products in the world, attacking not only tobacco, cigars and cigarettes but also aniseed, bamboo, beans, cassava, cocoa, coriander, cumin, dried bananas, medicinal drugs, flour, ginger, herbs, plant-derived insecticides such as pyrethrum, as well as juniper seed, paprika, potpourri, pinned insects, rhubarb, spices and yeast, dried fish, stored wax, cloth, paper, books and even wood.

Yes, the beetle can bore its way into and out of a box of cigars. It owes its omnivorous habits in part to a symbiotic B vitamin–producing yeast that lives inside it, which enables the beetle to supplement its diet and survive on foods that are poor in nutrients. So essential is this yeast that a female will pass it on to her young, coating it onto her eggs as they pass through her oviducts. The larvae will consume it during the process of hatching.

The cigarette beetle is small, brown and unobtrusive; just one-eighth of an inch long. If disturbed, it will tuck its head under its hoodlike pronotum, the body segment behind its head, giving it a hunched-back appearance. Such shrinking-violet habits make adults and eggs hard to detect, especially when they are accidentally incorporated into expensive tobacco products. What is that popping sound one hears as one gently puffs on that Cuban cigar? Maybe it is exploding insect exoskeletons, which rupture when the body fluids of trapped dead beetles heat up and expand.

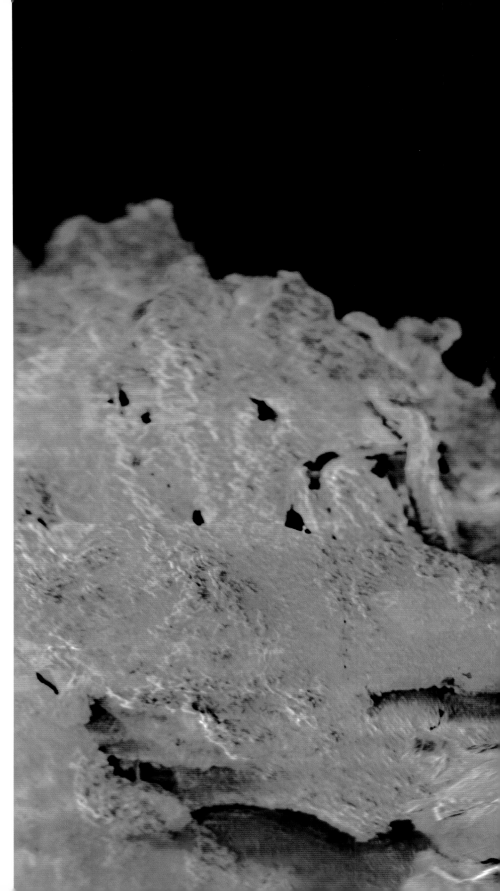

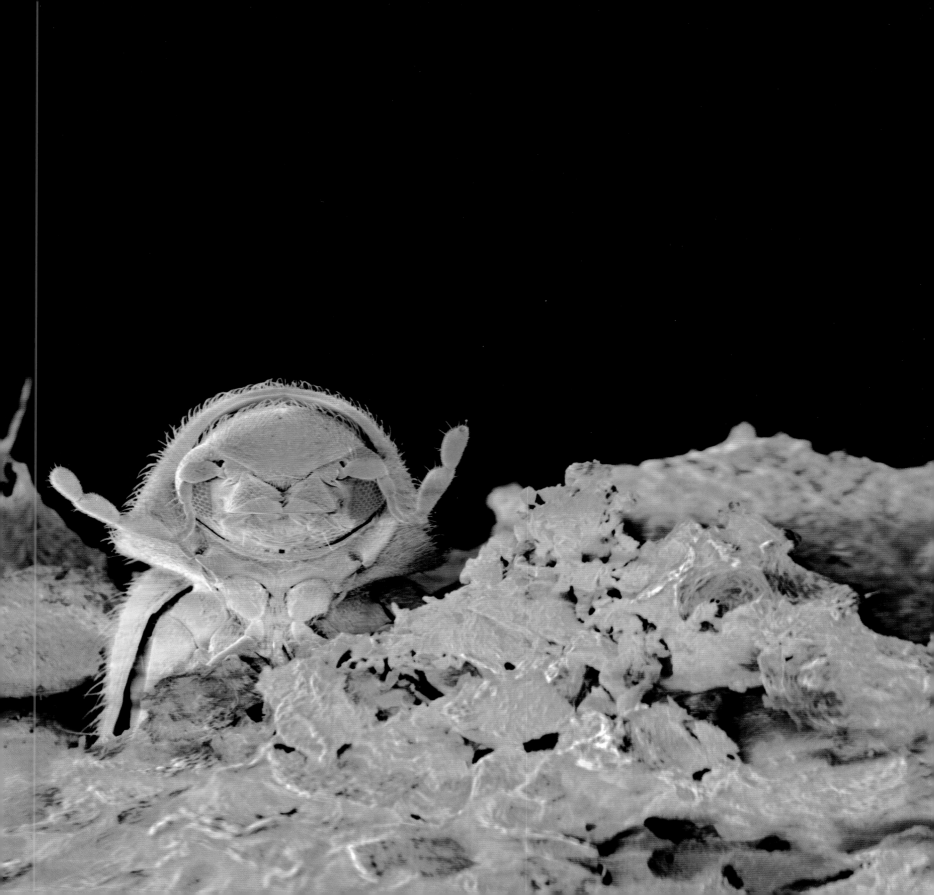

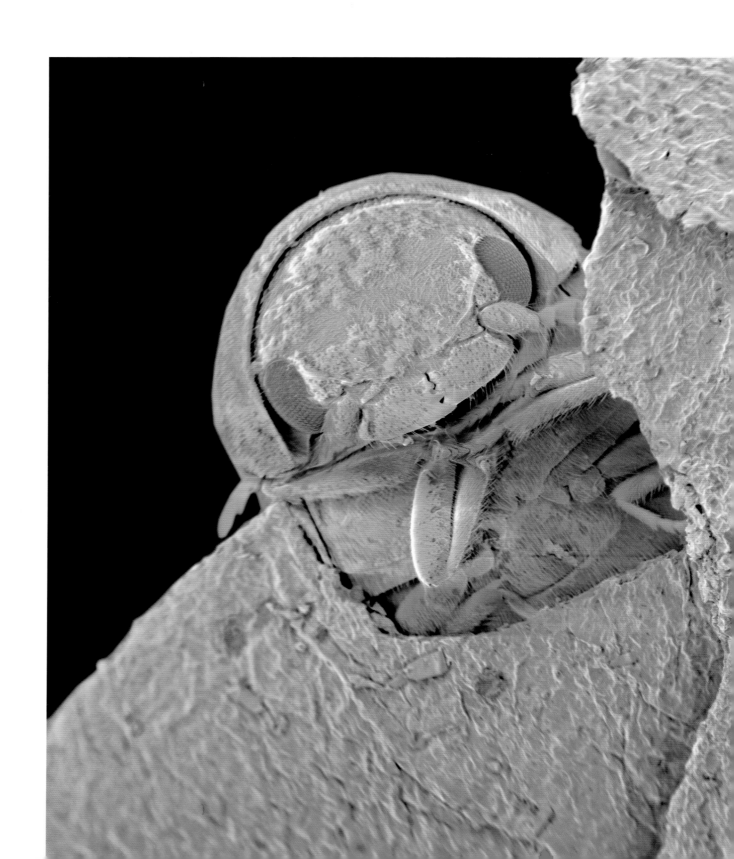

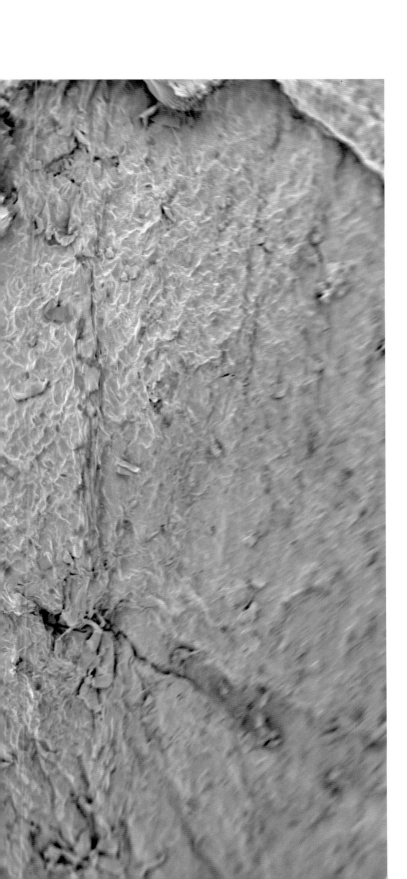

DRUGSTORE BEETLE
Stegobium paniceum

The drugstore beetle is a close relative of the cigarette beetle and, like its cousin, tends to tuck its head away if troubled by busybody humans. The word *stegos* is Latin for "hidden" and here it is, hiding behind a bread crumb. As its common name implies, the drugstore beetle is rather fond of mildly toxic medicines. It's rather keen on a lot of items: bread, books, flour, herbs and spices, fish food, even tin, aluminum foil and lead sheets—"anything but cast iron," as one wag put it.

SAWTOOTHED GRAIN BEETLE
Oryzaephilus surinamensis

The sawtoothed grain beetle is a straggler, it shows up when the party's half over. *Oryzaephilus surinamensis*, a rice lover from Suriname, doesn't eat whole seeds— or whole rice grains like this one on which it is perched—but it does gnaw on the surface of food after other insects have attacked it, leaving it pitted and scarred. *Oryzaephilus* infestations are obvious; these small, slim, flattened red beetles can be seen scuttling around on the surface of their favorite foods, which include almost all grains, dried fruits, nuts, sugar, dried meat and snuff. Their flattened forms enable them to crawl into extremely narrow spaces—such as the near-tight seals on packages of food.

NORTHERN SPIDER BEETLE
Mezium affine

Dead wood, mammal dung, bird debris— these are the preferred foods of the spider beetle, an insect that once spent its life scavenging in nature. Perhaps first introduced into stored grain facilities in the wood used to build them, now it forages on human foods. Despite its fearsome features, the spider beetle is not a monstrous pest, but it can survive and even thrive in freezing temperatures, making it common in unheated warehouses in winter, especially in the northern United States and Canada. Though it will willingly eat half-chewed grain left behind by more important pests such as *Sitophilus*, the spider beetle is often content to sample less nutritious fare— even rat droppings, if all else is lacking.

MEDICINE

BUGS THAT HARM, BUGS THAT HEAL

Blood, red blood
Super-magical
Forbidden liquor.

I behold you stand
For a second enspasmed in oblivion,
Obscenely ecstasied
Sucking live blood
My blood.

Such silence, such suspended transport,
Such gorging,
Such obscenity of trespass.

D. H. Lawrence, "The Mosquito" (1923)

The history of the world, as written by humans, is a battle-filled one, concerned above all with the rise and fall of empires, the conquest of continents, the accession and execution of kings and queens, as well as with revolution, renaissance, the flowering of art, culture and literature. Insects do not feature prominently in these chronicles. That is a shame, for insects and the diseases they transmit have had more influence over the course of human affairs than most historians care to acknowledge. It was fleas that carried the Black Death, a fourteenth-century plague that by one estimate killed about one-quarter of the entire European population, or some twenty-five million people. In its wake, agricultural land was redistributed, now-scarce workers struck for higher wages, universities closed and a new religious movement, the Flagellants, spread across Europe. Jews, accused of poisoning wells, were persecuted, burned and banished.

Yet plague is hardly the only insect-borne illness to have had a profound impact on human history. "Swords and lances, arrows, machine guns, and even high explosives have had far less power over the fates of nations than the typhus louse, the plague flea, and the yellow-fever mosquito," wrote Hans Zinsser in his rambling 1935 treatise *Rats, Lice and History*. "Civilizations have retreated from the plasmodium of malaria [. . .] and huge areas have been devastated by the trypanosome that travels on the wings of the tsetse fly." It was "General Typhus," along with "General Famine and General Winter," in the words of French Marshal Michel Ney, that defeated Napoleon's Grand Army, killing hundreds of thousands of soldiers on their ill-fated 1812 march on Moscow. And, until the discovery of quinine, mosquito-borne malaria largely prevented the exploration of Africa's interior by European explorers—who died from the disease in such high numbers that the west coast of Africa was dubbed "the white man's grave."

Even today, insect-borne diseases afflict vast swaths of humanity. Malaria still kills between one million and three million people every year, 90 percent of them in Africa south of the Sahara. Half a million people in Africa suffer from sleeping sickness, caused by a parasite called *Trypanosoma brucei* that is transmitted by the bite of the tsetse fly. Cone-nosed bugs in Central and South America pass on a related parasite, *Trypanosoma cruzi*, that causes deadly Chagas' disease. Eighteen million people in Africa are infected with onchocerciasis, or river blindness, caused by a parasitic worm injected by black flies. Leishmaniasis, transmitted by sand flies; elephantiasis, carried by mosquitoes; and trachoma, spread in part by eye-seeking flies, still infect tens of millions on all continents. And Lyme disease, transmitted not by insects but by eight-legged arachnid ticks, is a major cause of concern in the United States.

Strange to relate, then, that throughout history people have also turned to insects to cure diseases. To be sure, much of what passed for medicine in earlier times is now regarded as quackery. "To promote obstructed or retained urine, the following is a well-proven experiment," wrote Matthaeus Wagner in *The Traveling Samaritan, or the Short Pharmacopoeia of Good and Proven Medicinal Preparations*, published in 1685. "Take a good portion of Bedbugs or Wall-lice; let them boil in Olive Oil, and then allow the male privy parts to depend therein, as hot as can be borne." Hairy insects, like bees and flies, were touted as a remedy for baldness by, among others, Pliny the Elder, who recommended that the fly heads be first mixed with breast milk before being rubbed "in the bare places where the hair is gone." Singing insects like cicadas were commonly used to cure earache in Japan and China. And cantharidin, an extremely toxic extract of the metallic-blue beetle *Lytta vesicatoria*, was prescribed until the turn of the twentieth century for ailments ranging from carbuncles to catarrh. (It was also considered an aphrodisiac.)

Insect medicine cannot be entirely dismissed, however. One of the most unusual—and apparently highly effective—forms of bug surgery is found in India and South America, where the powerful mandibles of soldier ants and carpenter ants have been used for centuries to suture wounds. Bee venom therapy, a popular old remedy, has been revived in recent years for the treatment of inflammatory diseases such as rheumatoid arthritis. Honey, too, has potent antibacterial properties; recent research suggests that it is capable of killing antibiotic-resistant bacteria such as *Staphylococcus aureus*, indicating a possible role for it in treating wounds colonized by such microbes.

The emergence of antibiotic resistance has led to the resurgence of yet another unusual entomological cure: Maggot therapy, or the use of blowfly larvae to treat hard-to-heal ulcers, abscesses, gangrene and burns. The beneficial effects of such larvae—which eat dead flesh and ignore healthy tissue—were first noted by the sixteenth-century French surgeon Ambroise Paré, who noted that battlefield wounds healed faster when infested with maggots. Hundreds of doctors throughout the world now treat wounds with these larvae, with remarkable success.

Neither has extract of insect gone entirely out of fashion. One enterprising French company, the Strasbourg-based Entomed, is analyzing bugs around the globe in search of novel antibiotics and anticancer agents. Entocosm, in Australia, has a similar mission. Many insects manufacture all manner of compounds to fend off attacks from microorganisms, and both companies hope to co-opt these chemicals to fight human diseases. Entocosm has isolated several novel antibacterial compounds from the cathedral termite, *Nasutitermes triodiae*, whose caste of defensive "soldiers" squirt a cocktail of antibiotic chemicals from a nozzle in the middle of their heads. Meanwhile Entomed has screened more than one hundred butterflies, beetles, bees, ladybugs, cockroaches and flies for medicinal material and has several products now in clinical testing. Perhaps they will prove more effective than elixir of bedbug or fly head.

BODY LOUSE
Pediculus humanus corporis

A sign, spotted atop a pile of possessions sitting on a street in downtown Manhattan:

> *Leave my stuff alone!*
> *I went to the bathroom & my stuff has*
> *several species of LICE!*
> *So don't pick it up*
> *I'll be right back*
> *I'm probably coming down the street*
> *right now looking at you!*

There are, in fact, three species of lice that call humans their home: the crab louse, which lives only among pubic hairs; the head louse; and its descendent, pictured here, the body louse, *Pediculus humanus corporis*, which probably took up residence in garments only after humans began wearing them. They leave them only to feed on blood and after death, when the body cools. One famous louse host was Thomas à Becket, murdered in Canterbury Cathedral in 1170 by henchmen of England's King Henry II. As his robe-swaddled body lay in state the next day, onlookers were alternately aghast, then convulsed with laughter,

to see that "the vermin boiled over like water in a simmering cauldron."

These body lice are boiling over with something else: lust. Caught *in flagrante*, they would—had they been left in peace—have later stuck their eggs, or nits, to the fibers found in clothes. The nymphs that hatch out cannot survive in unworn clothing; hence, body lice are most frequently transmitted in crowded conditions like prison camps, where bathing is infrequent and clothes cannot be changed. That could also explain why the diseases they transmit in their feces—typhus, trench fever and relapsing fever—occur so commonly in wartime. Typhus, a disease caused by bacteria called rickettsias, has been blamed for numerous military debacles, the earliest in 1489 when "malignant spotted fever" killed 17,000 soldiers in a war over Granada between the Moors and the Spanish army of Ferdinand and Isabella. Typhus claimed so many millions of lives during the Bolshevik Revolution that it threatened to torpedo the newborn Soviet state, leading Lenin to exclaim, "Either socialism will defeat the louse, or the louse will defeat socialism."

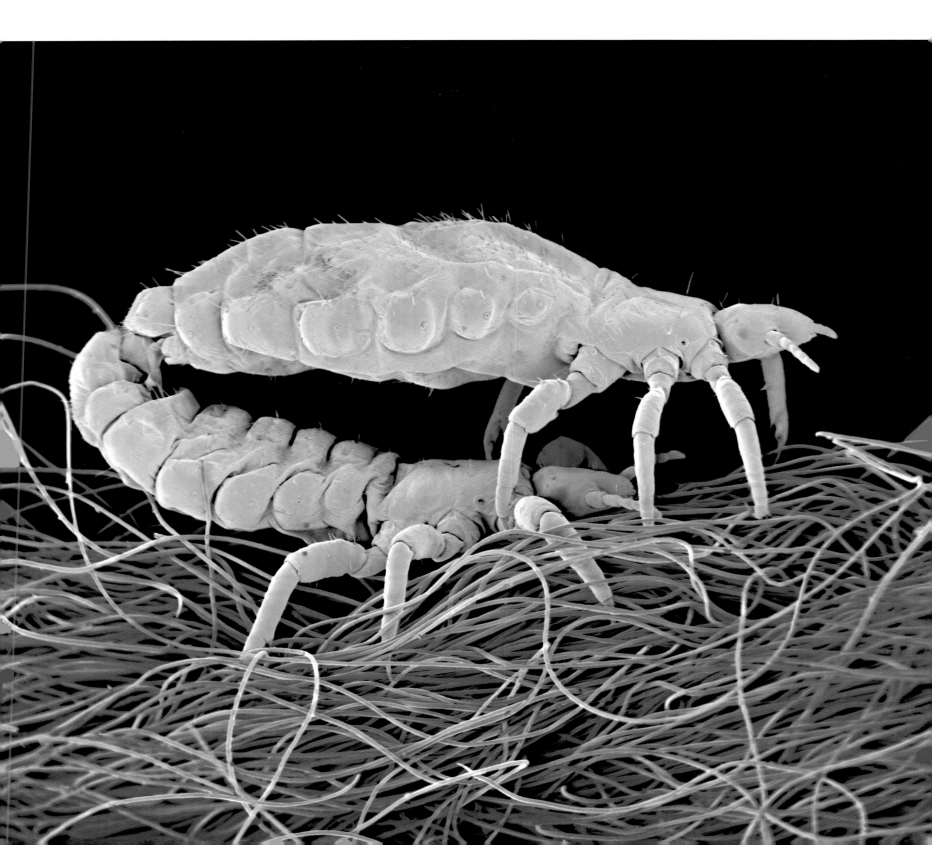

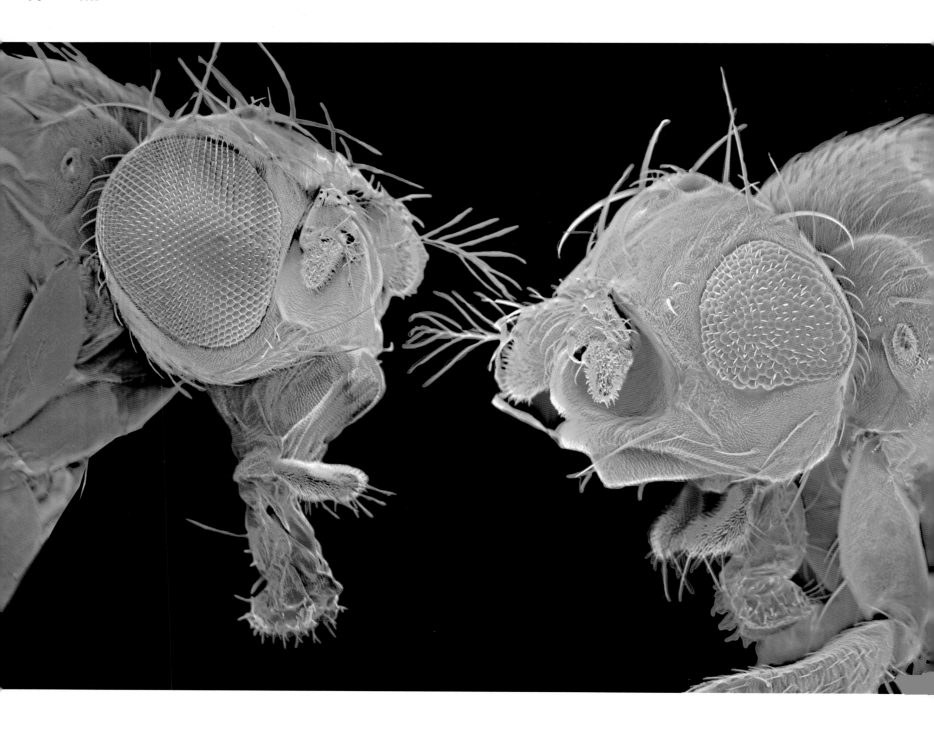

FRUIT FLY
Drosophila melanogaster

Methuselah, dachshund, forkhead, amnesiac, radish and *cabbage, I'm not dead yet*—just a few of the names that have adorned the myriad mutants of this unassuming insect, whose real name is *Drosophila melanogaster*, Latin for *black-bellied dew lover*, or plain old fruit fly in common parlance. Had it not been for Thomas Hunt Morgan, a zoologist who in 1909 adopted the fruit fly as a model genetic organism, the fruit fly might have languished in obscurity, hopping about among the banana peels in the garbage bin or getting quietly drunk during the grape harvest. Morgan showed that string-like structures called chromosomes sitting inside the fly's cells carry instructions—genes—that can be swapped around by sexual reproduction to produce new and unique combinations. Since then scientists have zapped the fly with X rays to produce bizarre mutants, mapped all of its genes, and analyzed it inside-out for clues to human diseases.

Using a fast-breeding fly as a model for human medicine is not as strange as it sounds. For example, biologists at the University of California, San Diego, have identified genes in fruit flies that are counterparts of those that cause more than 700 different genetic diseases in humans, among them immunological, cardiovascular and neurological disorders. Cancer, drug addiction, alcoholism and jet lag are all human ailments that have found analogs among fruit fly variants. The *blue cheese* gene, for example, is a mutation that triggers adult fruit flies to develop signs of Alzheimer's—protein plaques that transform the brain into a mass resembling a moldy and marbled cheese. *Methuselah* and *I'm not dead yet* are flies that live well beyond their appointed days, suggesting a prominent role for them in studies of aging. *Amnesiac* is the idiot fly, as are *radish* and *cabbage*; they are unable to perform simple memory tests that other flies learn easily. These three were bred for behavior research, but who knows what twisted human mind produced the stubby-legged *dachshund*; or *forkhead*, which has head parts where its gut ought to be?

CHAGAS' DISEASE VECTOR
Rhodnius prolixus

"It is most disgusting to feel soft wingless insects, about an inch long, crawling over one's body. Before sucking they are quite thin, but afterwards they become round and bloated with blood, and in this state are easily crushed." Thus wrote Charles Darwin in *The Voyage of the Beagle*, describing an attack in Argentina one night in 1835 by "the great black bug of the Pampas." That biter may well have been a relative of this bloodsucking beast, a cone-nosed bug named *Rhodnius prolixus*, the vector of a protozoan parasite called *Trypanosoma cruzi* that causes Chagas' disease. Indeed, within two years of returning home to England, Darwin developed a mysterious life-long malaise with symptoms similar to those elicited by Chagas'; vomiting, violent shivering, lassitude and a "swimmy" head. That his doctors were unable to diagnose the cause is not surprising, the disease was not described until 1910, when a Brazilian doctor named Carlos Chagas dissected a number of cone-nosed bugs and found their hindguts swimming with single-celled trypanosomes.

Chagas was convinced that the bugs transmit the disease through a bite. It turns out that it is not their mouthparts but their rear ends that are responsible—parasites in their feces, deposited during feeding, are carried into the body when a victim of their bite scratches or rubs the wound. From there they are free to invade muscle and nerve cells, causing chills, anemia, muscle and bone pain, or, in the chronic form of the disease, progressive weakness and an enlarged, flabby heart prone to sudden failure. Between sixteen and eighteen million people in Central and South America are still infected each year with Chagas' disease, 21,000 of whom—mostly the poorest of the poor—will die. Drugs are often ineffective and frequently unaffordable, so control of the disease has focused instead on eliminating the bug from its daytime indoor hidey-holes: cracks, crevices and thatch. Venezuela and Colombia, for example, have begun campaigns to replace palm-roofed, adobe-walled huts with zinc-roofed, plaster-walled houses. The World Health Organization hopes to eliminate the disease by 2010.

EUROPEAN HONEYBEE HATCHING
Apis mellifera

Of all the insects flying about the earth, the honeybee is probably best beloved by humans. The feeling is probably not mutual, since humans have been helping themselves to honey and beeswax for at least three thousand years, when they first domesticated the bee. According to one estimate, approximately one-third of the human diet is now derived directly or indirectly from bee-pollinated crops. Were bees to disappear—driven extinct, say, by indiscriminate insecticide use—we would likely lose from our diet almonds, oranges, eggplants, tea, garlic, onions and carrots, among others.

Not only as a food source, though, have humans exploited bees like this one, seen here poking out its proboscis as it hatches from a honeycomb. Bee venom has long been known to soothe arthritis, probably because it contains melittin, one of the most potent anti-inflammatory agents known. Many other bee venom components have medicinal qualities: Adolapin, for example, is a painkiller; apamin is said to enhance nerve transmission, and several enzymes in it have antifungal and antibacterial effects. Injected beneath the skin, bee venom extract may alleviate such chronic conditions as multiple sclerosis, psoriasis and lupus, and it can also soften scar tissue. Honey, too, has proven antibacterial activities. In recent research conducted at the University of Wales, honey was shown to be ten times more effective than an artificial sugar solution at killing antibiotic-resistant *Staphylococcus aureus*, a wound-infecting bacteria now common in hospitals, perhaps because it contains plant chemicals and enzymes that inhibit bacterial growth. The finding suggests that honey could provide a cheap future alternative to increasingly ineffective antibiotics.

Bees may be able to protect human health in one other, highly unusual, way. Using sugar as a reward, scientists at the U.S. Department of Defense have trained honeybees to detect minute traces of explosives. As sensitive to odors as dogs, and even more dogged in following a fine molecular trail, the bees may one day be used to expose truck bombs, landmines or other concealed ammunition.

MAGGOT
Lucilia sericata

The sight of small maggots wriggling around in a wound is enough to send some timid souls screaming away in horror. Not William Baer. During World War I, this orthopedic surgeon had the opportunity to examine two soldiers who had been left for seven days, injured and without food or water, in an area of the battlefield obscured by brush. "On removing the clothing from the wounded part, much was my surprise to see the wound filled with thousands and thousands of maggots, apparently those of the blow fly," he wrote. Even more astonishing, though, was that the soldiers' injuries were almost healed, "filled with the most beautiful pink granulation tissue one could imagine." Baer had stumbled upon a phenomenon first observed by sixteenth-century French surgeon Ambroise Paré: Maggots, by eating away at dead tissue, can heal wounds that might otherwise fester.

Baer later pioneered the use of green blowfly larvae—Lucilia sericata, such as this one—for treating osteomyelitis, a chronic bone infection. By the mid-1940s, maggot therapy for infected wounds and abscesses was routinely performed at over 300 hospitals in the United States. Though they were abandoned with the advent of antibiotics, maggots are now enjoying a weird renaissance, impelled in part by the rise of bacterial resistance to antibiotics. The maggot's secret lies in its secretions; powerful protein-digesting enzymes, antibiotics that pulverize all manner of microorganisms, and growth factors that promote tissue repair. To many people suffering from intractable, hard-to-treat wounds—diabetic foot ulcers, abscesses and gangrene—maggots are medical saviors, through their relentless chewing saving limbs that might otherwise be lost to amputation. Their other advantage lies in the fact that maggots eat only dead tissue and not healthy flesh, dropping off wounds to pupate when they are full. A recent University of California, Irvine, study of maggot therapy shows how effective it is—maggot-treated pressure ulcers were more likely to heal, and did so far faster, than those wrapped only with conventional dressings.

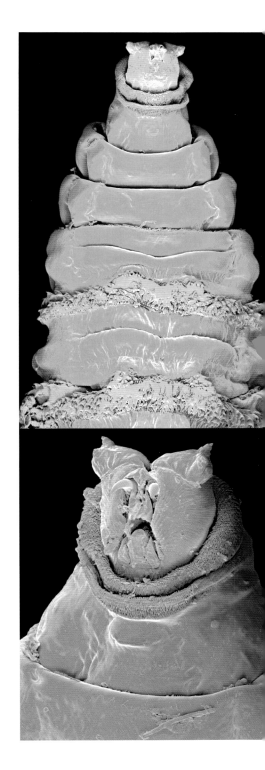

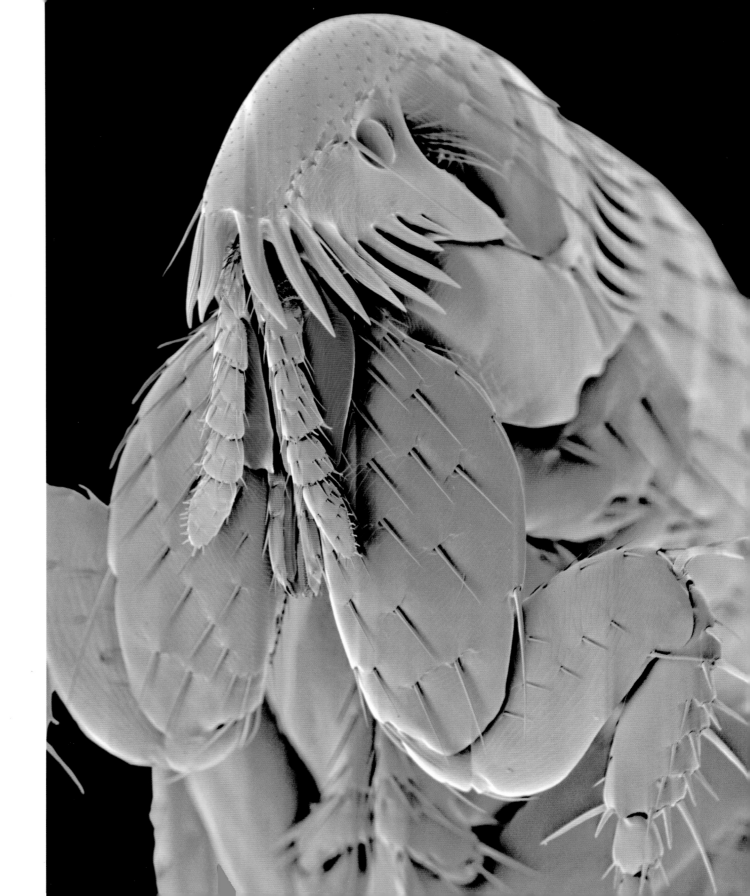

CAT FLEA
Ctenocephalides felis

The education of a seventeenth-century French princess once included the following dictum: "It was bad manners to scratch when one did it by habit and not by necessity, and [. . .] it was improper to take lice or fleas or other vermin by the neck to kill them in company, except in the most intimate circles." This advice on etiquette was presumably directed at the human flea, *Pulex irritans*, and not at this one, which is a cat flea, or *Ctenocephalides felis*. It hardly matters in any case, since cat fleas readily feed on humans, too, as well as on dogs and chickens.

As parasites, fleas have few peers. Champion jumpers, both human and cat fleas can leap thirteen inches into the air to catch hold of a new host, the equivalent of a 6-foot human springing over an 800-foot high jump. They are also champion suckers, with sharp mouthparts equipped to cut and pierce the skin to siphon blood. In fact, only the adults are bloodsuckers; young larvae hang about in the nest or in bedding, chewing on cat flea feces or dried blood discharged by adults from their anuses while feeding.

Few insects can lay claim to changing human history. Fleas can. Transmitter of the plague bacterium, *Yersinia pestis*, the rat flea *Xenopsylla cheopis* has indirectly caused the deaths of millions, most famously during the medieval Black Death but also during repeated outbreaks that continued into the twentieth century. Yet for hundreds of years its victims were ignorant of the cause, often attributing plague to divine wrath. Not until 1897 did the true cause become clear, when Paul-Louis Simond found the plague bacillus in the stomachs of fleas taken from infected rats. Though the disease is now rare, it still surfaces from time to time, and there are disturbing reports that the bacillus is becoming resistant to antibiotics. Maybe the day will return when we will once again be forced to wear flea traps, such as the one fitted in 1784 with a small microscope with which to examine the captured prey. "Many a demoiselle wears this gadget hung around her neck between the *duplex genus feminum*," read the directions.

MOSQUITO
Anopheles stephensi

Elegant, dainty and deadly, *Anopheles stephensi* is one of seventy species of mosquito able to transmit malaria, a scourge that has menaced humans since at least 1550 B.C.E., when the Egyptian Ebers papyrus first described its fever. Malaria—from the word meaning "bad air"—has been linked throughout history to marshes, but it was not until 1897 that surgeon Ronald Ross was able to prove that mosquitoes, which breed in swamps and puddles, were vectors of the malaria parasite. Dissecting some "dappled-winged" *Anopheles* mosquitoes that had fed on a malaria patient in India, Ross found the parasite, a protozoan named *Plasmodium*, growing in the insects' guts. "God hath put into my hand a wondrous thing," he wrote in his notebook. "At this command I have found thy secret deeds, Oh million-murdering Death."

Ross was convinced that his discovery would save "a myriad men," and he may have been right—for a time. A mass mosquito eradication campaign using the pesticide DDT was launched in 1955, and by 1961 had eliminated or dramatically reduced the incidence of malaria in thirty-seven countries. But mosquito resistance to DDT developed rapidly, and today the disease is still endemic in much of sub-Saharan Africa, where one child dies of malaria every thirty seconds. There is no vaccine against it, and drugs to combat the malaria parasite have run into similar resistance.

So scientists have turned to a high-tech approach. In 2002, they announced that they had genetically modified *Anopheles stephensi*, an Indian species of the mosquito, so that it could no longer transmit mouse malaria. The mosquito carries an antiparasitic protein that probably blocks invasion of *Plasmodium* into its gut, where the pathogen must multiply before migrating into the insect's salivary glands, ready to infect the next human it bites. In theory such modified mosquitoes, if released into the wild, could replace their more deadly malaria-transmitting cousins—a strategy that has yet to be proven effective. In the same year, though, two other teams sequenced the genomes of both *Plasmodium falciparum*, the most malignant malaria parasite, as well as *Anopheles gambiae*, its principal carrier. Among the intriguing findings: A novel set of smell receptors that could explain the mosquito's penchant for human blood. The discovery may enable researchers to design novel repellents to combat malaria and other mosquito-borne diseases.

MOSQUITO

Anopheles stephensi

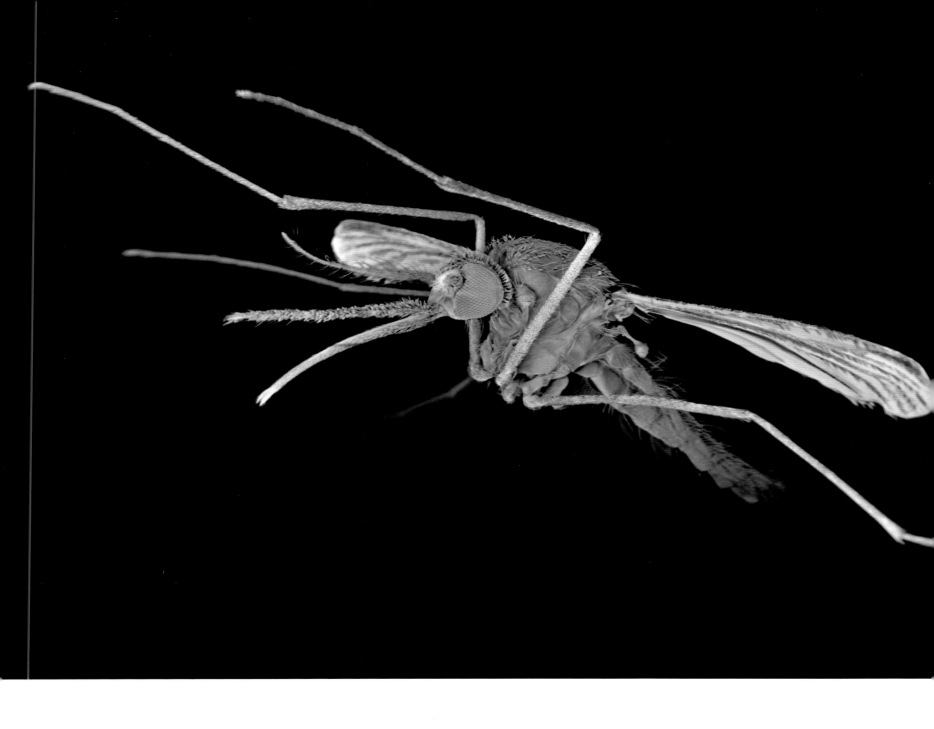

MOSQUITO
Culex pipiens

In the summer of 1999, a dead Chilean flamingo was discovered in New York's Bronx Zoo. The bird was later found to be carrying West Nile virus, the cause of a brain inflammation that has since sickened thousands and killed almost three hundred people in the United States. The vector of the West Nile virus is this bird-feeding mosquito called *Culex pipiens*. As a result of the initial epidemic—which also killed a lot of crows—epidemiologists fanned out across New York City in search of the virus in wintering adult *Culex* mosquitoes, which seek out still, moist spots in which to hibernate during cold months. They looked under bridges and in tunnels, in abandoned buildings and even in a Civil War–era fort and found the virus inside a few specimens— indicating that West Nile would probably return the following spring.

In order to eliminate or reduce the incidence of the disease, scientists have to strike where the larvae are known to develop: sewers, storm-water outflows, swimming pools and puddles. Unless such breeding sites are eradicated or treated with mosquito larvicides, there can be no hope

of controlling the insect—or the pathogens it carries. Mosquitoes favor pools of standing water because that is where they lay their eggs, which hatch into larvae called wigglers. The wigglers are suspended from the surface of the water by an air tube through which they breathe. The pupae they grow into are called tumblers, after the tumbling motion with which they swim to the bottom of their pool if disturbed. To breathe, they break through the surface with the aid of a pair of trumpet-shaped tubes on their thorax. Larvae live about two weeks in the water before emerging as adults.

Is there anyone, or anything, that actually *likes* mosquitoes? Well, some bats and birds eat them. And certain species of fish feed on them, which makes the fish good biological control agents in rice paddies. A. B. Rich, author of *Our Near Neighbor the Mosquito*, a slim compendium published in 1901, wrote that "we cannot fail to be impressed . . . by their infinite numbers, emerging from the shores of the ocean, the banks of all streams, shallow waters, marshes and jungles of the forests." He did not include the London Underground, in which a new species of rodent-feeding mosquito was recently found to have evolved—descendents of bird-biting *C. pipiens* that colonized the tunnels more than a century ago.

DOG TICKS MATING
Ixodes ricinus

Connubial bliss for this pair of dog ticks is a complicated affair. That wee male is inserting his mouthparts, called chelicerae, deep down into the genital pore of his massive mate, a female tick bloated after a blood meal. He does this to detect and identify pheromones signaling her readiness to reproduce. When he is done sniffing, he will withdraw his mouthparts and shift them towards his own genital opening in order to grab an emerging bag of sperm, called a spermatophore, that he will edge inside the female. She will then fall off her host, lay thousands of eggs, and die.

Ticks' mating and egg-laying habits are of more than passing interest to biologists largely because of the wide range of diseases they carry. These eight-legged, bloodsucking arachnids transmit the microbial agents that cause Lyme disease, Rocky Mountain spotted fever, tularemia and Q fever, among others. Not all tick species carry the same pathogens. These conjoined creatures are *Ixodes ricinus*, a European species known variously as dog ticks, sheep ticks or castor bean ticks. The names are

misleading, because *I. ricinus* can feed on more than two hundred hosts, primarily rodents and ruminants but also, on occasion, humans. It is a known vector of *Borrelia burgdorferi*, the bacteria that causes Lyme disease; *Babesia*, a microscopic protozoan parasite that infects red blood cells; *Bartonella henselae*, the bacterial cause of cat-scratch disease, as well as viral encephalitis.

Given the threat ticks pose to humans, scientists are always on the lookout for innovative methods of controlling them. One such technique has focused on the aphrodisiacs that draw these mating arachnids together. Parasitologist Daniel Sonenshine of Old Dominion University in Norfolk, Virginia, has even patented a "tick decoy" shaped like a satiated female tick that is impregnated with a pheromone and a tick-killing acaricide. The device not only draws sex-hungry males toward it but kills them most efficiently, leaving any remaining females lacking mates. A modified, flea-collar-type version of the decoy has even been attached to the tails of cattle in Africa to help them fight off bont ticks, which transmit a deadly disease known as heartwater.

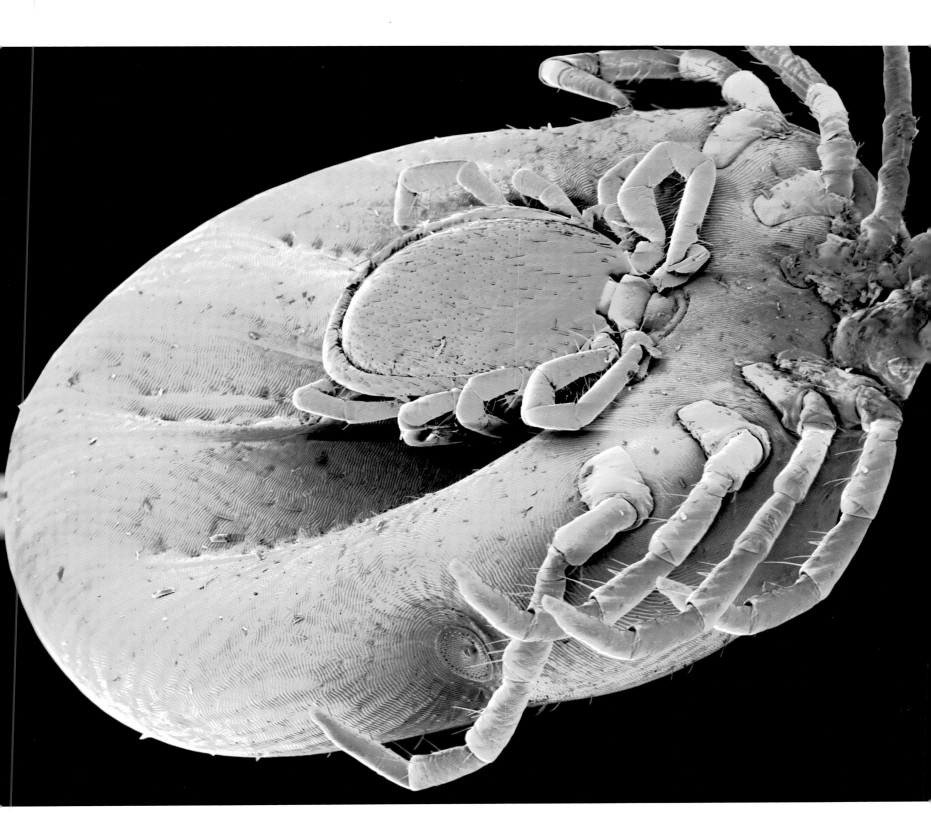

TICK FEEDING ON THE SKIN OF A MOUSE
Ixodes ricinus

The tick is an unusually compact animal. Not for the separate head, thorax and abdomen found in insects; instead, all three are fused into one. In place of a head, the tick has a capitulum, a complex feeding organ superbly adapted for sucking blood. A pair of pedipalps grasps a fold of skin while cutting tools called chelicerae slice into it; then a barbed appendage called a hypostome, which helps anchor the tick to its host, is thrust into the wound. Blood and lymph from the slashed tissues well into the gash, and the tick laps them up. Hard ticks like this mouse-feeding *Ixodes ricinus* can stay gorging on blood for days before detaching.

All *Ixodes* ticks are blind blood feeders, and they spread a greater variety of diseases than any other bloodsucking animal, including mosquitoes. One of these is Lyme disease, caused by the bacteria *Borrelia burgdorferi* and transmitted on the eastern coast of North America by the black-legged tick, *Ixodes scapularis*, and on the Pacific coast by *Ixodes pacificus*. The black-legged deer tick has a complex life cycle, with adults feeding on large mammals such as deer and humans, and larvae and nymphs biting mice and other rodents as well as small birds. Preventing Lyme disease—an arthritis-like illness that first surfaced in the town of Lyme, Connecticut, in 1977—depends upon reducing exposure to infected ticks. But this isn't as easy as it sounds. As the suburbs creep inexorably into the woods, more people are exposed to these pinhead-sized biters.

In fact, recent research shows that as forest fragmentation rises, so too does the risk of contracting Lyme disease. With fewer predators to feed upon them, white footed mice—the principal carriers of Lyme bacteria—can run amok in small forest patches. So scientists are turning to other methods of controlling the disease. University of Rhode Island researchers, for example, hope to develop a vaccine against the tick's saliva, which they collect by inducing the ticks, with the aid of a muscle relaxant, to drool into a tube. Tick saliva contains over four hundred proteins that suppress blood clotting, increase the flow of blood to the bite, and battle the mammal host's immune response. By designing a vaccine against one or more of these proteins, the Rhode Island team hopes to interrupt transmission of the disease. So far, they have collected more tick saliva than any other set of scientists anywhere in the world.

DELUSORY PARASITOSIS

In a recent global survey, scientists at the London School of Hygiene and Tropical Medicine asked respondents in five different countries to describe what most disgusts them. The lists they compiled included prominent mention of insects—flies, maggots, lice, "cockroaches in my bed" or "millions of bugs clustered together" to cite some examples. Sadly, some people simply don't like insects. Others go further. They believe that they are not only surrounded by bugs—as we all are—but that their skin, hair, nose or ears are being invaded by mites, insects or even, in one instance, tiny lobsters. Such "delusions of parasitosis" were first described in the 1940s, and since then doctors have documented hundreds of cases.

The course of the delusion typically follows a standard pattern. Usually the "bugs" are black or white when first seen, but may later change color. They often jump or glide over the body, or crawl out of cosmetics, shampoo or toothpaste. "Bites" appear on the skin, often exacerbated by compulsive scratching or applications of insecticidal sprays. Sometimes the "invasion" may become so severe that the victim of such delusions moves to a new home—only to be followed by the "bugs" to the new abode. No doctor can dissuade the sufferer that the infestation is imaginary, despite the patient's repeated offerings of evidence of the insect influx—small bags or boxes containing scraps of skin, dried blood or nasal mucus, household dust and fluff or fragments of common, usually harmless, household insects. Sometimes the sufferers spend all their spare money on soaps, disinfectants or pesticides, or all of their spare time scrubbing and sterilizing their home, to no avail.

Unfortunately, the prognosis for delusory parasitosis is not a promising one. Dermatologists encountering such delusions often wish to refer such patients to psychiatrists, but just as often the patient refuses to go, preferring to believe that the infestation is real. A thorough examination of the person's home by a trained entomologist to rule out real infestations may help dispel the illusion. Failing that, antipsychotic drugs are often said to be effective.

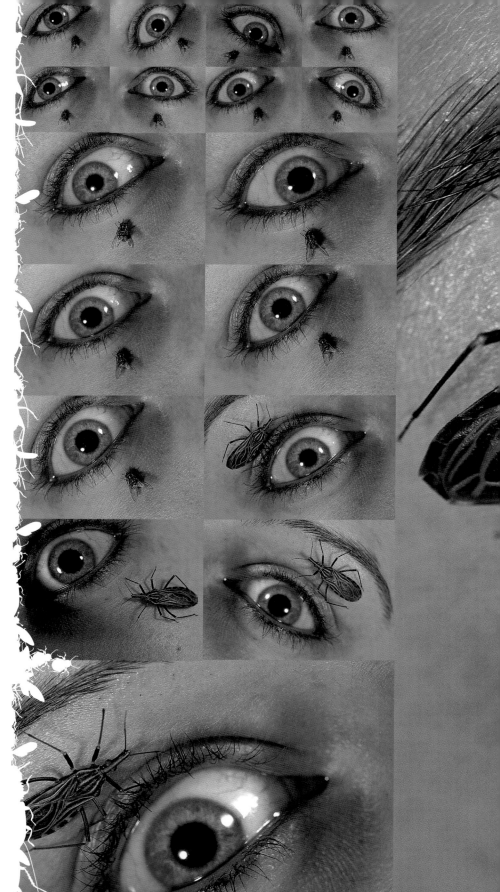

DRAWING BLOOD FROM A CASTNIID MOTH LARVA

For centuries quacks and apothecaries have offered insects as a cure for all kinds of ills. Oil of earwigs was thought to strengthen the nerves when smeared on the wrists and nostrils; ants in alcohol were a remedy for rheumatism; crushed cockroaches could cure dropsy, weak sight, ulcers and earache. *Pulvis dentrificius*, or pulverized ladybugs, were offered for toothache, measles and colic, and smoked locusts were recommended for urine retention. Twenty-first-century sophisticates may sneer at such medicaments, but scientists at Entomed, a French company based in Strasbourg, think bugs are an untapped source of drugs. For the past few years, they have been gathering insects from around the world and extracting their hemolymph—the blood that bathes all the tissues in the insect's body cavity—in search of new antibiotics, as well as new anti-inflammatory, antiviral and anticancer drugs.

Their quest is not all that odd. Insects, living in all sorts of environments—the rain forest floor, the insides of sewers, pools of petroleum—are exposed to all manner of microbes. To combat them they have, over their 500 million years of existence, evolved a powerful immune response consisting of peptides and small molecules to fight off microbial attack. To harvest such protective particles, scientists at Entomed inundate the insects with a cocktail of noxious bacteria and fungi to trigger an immune response. Then they siphon off their hemolymph, as this technician can be seen doing to a moth larva discovered inside a palm tree in French Guiana. So far they have screened more than one hundred butterflies, beetles, bees, ladybugs, cockroaches and flies, from which they have analyzed over 175 novel molecules with potential medical effects. One such substance, an antifungal agent based on a peptide found in the butterfly *Heliothis virescens*, has already undergone clinical trials for treatment of immunosuppressed patients suffering from hard-to-treat, hospital-acquired fungal infections.

Gathered in French Guiana, these are some of the insects under investigation by Entomed:

a DRUGS-FROM-BUGS BAZAAR

When Alexander Fleming discovered penicillin in 1928, he gave the world a wonder drug capable of conquering scourges such as syphilis, gangrene and tuberculosis. Unfortunately, bacterial resistance to the antibiotic began surfacing within four years of the start of its mass-production in 1943. Today about 70 percent of hospital-acquired bacterial infections are resistant to at least one of the drugs used to treat them, and some organisms are impervious to all approved antibiotics. Overuse and misuse of the drugs, as well as a certain microbial craftiness have all contributed to the problem. Most antibiotics target a specific enzyme or receptor involved in DNA or protein synthesis; by tweaking the enzyme slightly, bacteria can evade antibiotic attack.

Antimicrobial peptides extracted from insects have a different mode of action: They drill holes in the membranes of fungi and bacteria. Since it is very difficult for a microbe to change its entire cell wall, insect-derived antibiotics may be far less susceptible to bacterial resistance. They are also active against a wide range of microorganisms and have so far proved safe and nontoxic to mammals. Tens of millions of insect species on Earth may thus prove a potential treasure-house of undiscovered medicines, a case in point for preserving the natural habitats in which they dwell. "Biodiversity is our most valuable but least appreciated resource," writes biologist Edward O. Wilson. "A rare beetle sitting on an orchid in a remote valley of the Andes might secrete a substance that cures pancreatic cancer."

HARLEQUIN BEETLE
Acrocinus longimanus

"The *Arlequin* of Guiana, a gigantic mower" wrote Jules Michelet in his 1883 book *The Insect*, "armed with tremendous antennae and prodigious legs to traverse the innumerable obstacles offered by the tall herbage, is marked with black commas on a yellow ground, with inexplicable hieroglyphs—a being doubly strange and doubly enigmatic." This beetle's brightly colored back is, in fact, a form of camouflage. The long-horned, long-legged, Central American harlequin beetle lives hidden on mottled, lichen-covered trunks of hardwood trees, feeding on sap and laying its eggs on dead wood. This beetle is also home to a community of tiny arachnids called pseudoscorpions, which live nestled beneath its dazzling elytra, the tough modified forewings that protect the bodies of all beetles. These tiny pseudoscorpions use the harlequin beetle as a sort of transit plane to new locations, lassoing themselves to its abdomen with the aid of silken safety threads. When the beetle reaches a new log, its passengers slide off.

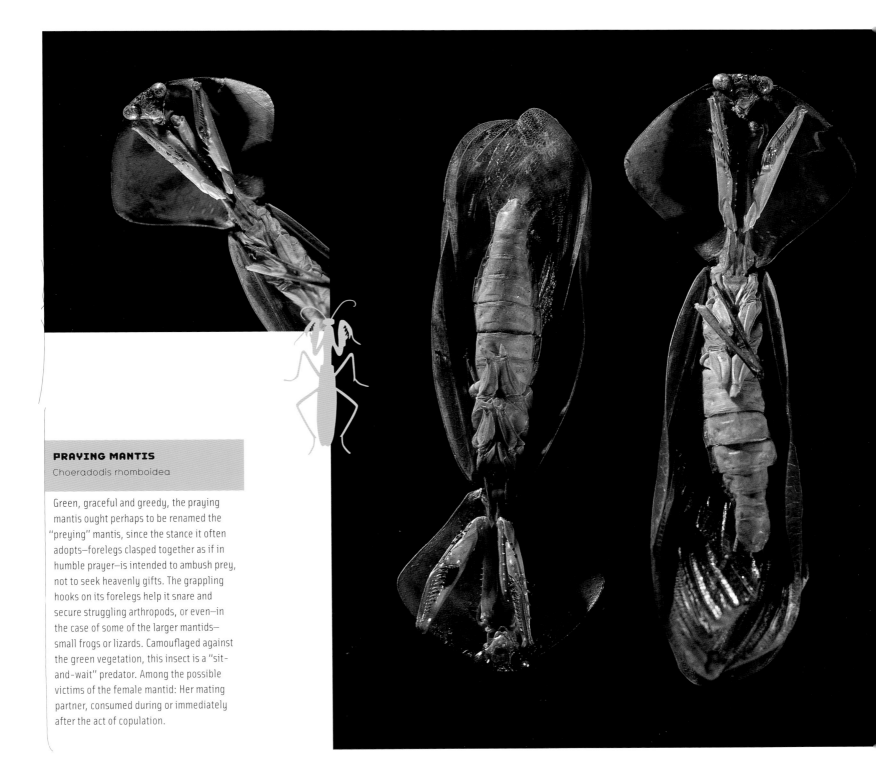

PRAYING MANTIS
Choeradodis rhomboidea

Green, graceful and greedy, the praying mantis ought perhaps to be renamed the "preying" mantis, since the stance it often adopts—forelegs clasped together as if in humble prayer—is intended to ambush prey, not to seek heavenly gifts. The grappling hooks on its forelegs help it snare and secure struggling arthropods, or even—in the case of some of the larger mantids—small frogs or lizards. Camouflaged against the green vegetation, this insect is a "sit-and-wait" predator. Among the possible victims of the female mantid: Her mating partner, consumed during or immediately after the act of copulation.

CICADA
Carineta aratayensis

Because of the cicada's unique lifestyle, the ancient Chinese considered it a symbol of rebirth. Living quietly underground—in some species for as long as seventeen years—cicadas emerge en masse to mate, lay eggs and die. Recent research suggests that root-feeding cicada nymphs time their emergence by monitoring the ebb and flow of sugars and proteins in the trees' sap each spring, counting each annual cycle until the requisite number of seasons has passed. Tree-living adult males are the drummers of the insect world, producing species-specific mating drones and whines with the aid of ribbed membranes, called tymbals, at the base of their abdomens.

CHRYSOMELID BEETLE
Platyphora aulica

The cautionary colors of this chrysomelid beetle—orange and metallic green—are intended as a warning to potential predators: Don't eat me. I taste *really* bad. Many of these lurid-hued leaf beetles harbor toxic molecules in their tissues that, once sampled by birds or lizards, are never forgotten. One species of chrysomelid beetle, from the genus *Diamphidia*, has even found a role in human hunting; some San people of the northern Kalahari extract a noxious substance from its larvae and pupae and smear it onto the ends of their arrows before shooting in order to paralyze their prey.

CONTROL

THE NEVER-ENDING BATTLE

On every dish the booming beetle falls,
The cockroach plays, or caterpillar crawls:
A thousand shapes of variegated hues
Parade the table and inspect the stews.
To living walls the swarming hundreds stick,
Or court, a dainty meal, the oily wick;
Heaps over heaps their slimy bodies drench,
Out go the lamps with suffocating stench.
When hideous insects every plate defile,
The laugh how empty, and how forced the smile!

"A Poet of the Indies"
from *The Insect Menace*
by Leland O. Howard
(1931)

Ever since humans began cultivating crops—about ten thousand years ago—they have had to share their hard-earned grains and beans and fruits with hordes of hungry insects. No wonder that they have spent equal time in a near-fruitless fight to eliminate these pests. But no incantation, potion or powder has ever been able to completely destroy these insatiable swarms, for insects are hardy survivors: they breed fast and frequently and have evolved to evade or resist even the most noxious of pesticides.

That insect pests have harassed humans since history was first recorded is without question. The Book of Exodus describes in vivid detail the plagues of lice, gnats and locusts visited upon the Egyptian oppressors of the Israelites; the locusts, says Exodus, *"covered the surface of the whole earth, so that the land was darkened, and they ate every plant of the land, and all the fruit of the trees [. . .] and there remained no green thing in the trees, or in the plants of the field, through all the land of Egypt."* Perhaps it was to protect themselves from a comparable plague of flies that the Philistines in the ancient land of Canaan appointed Beelzebub, or Ba'al Zevuv—Hebrew or Assyrian for "Lord of the Flies"—as their patron deity. Spells, magic and prayers formed the first line of attack against pests in much of the ancient world. The first-century Roman historian Pliny the Elder, for example, was convinced that leading a bare-breasted virgin around a hedge three times would force caterpillars to fall to the ground.

The Romans were familiar with the insecticidal properties of certain plants, such as cedar, wormwood, cumin, elder and asafetida. But it was not until the twentieth century that chemical warfare on insects began in earnest. Books like *The Insect Menace,* published in 1931 by Leland O. Howard, chief of the Bureau of Entomology at the U.S. Department of Agriculture, began warning of "mass starvation of humanity and the dominance of the insect type in this world" if people continued to ignore the threat that these troublesome arthropods posed to the global food supply. Howard must therefore have had cause to celebrate in 1939 when Swiss scientist Paul Hermann Müller discovered that DDT, a chemical

synthesized some sixty-five years earlier, was one of the most powerful and persistent insecticides ever invented. Soon it and other new chemical pesticides such as aldrin, dieldrin, and malathion were being sprayed in massive quantities to combat all manner of pests, from malaria-carrying mosquitoes to cotton bollworms and wood-eating termites.

And remarkably effective they were too—for a time. But soon problems began to appear. For one thing many populations of insects, including houseflies and mosquitoes, were evolving resistance to the insecticides, via gene mutations coding for enzymes that could, for example, detoxify DDT. For another, the chemicals were killing off beneficial insects such as predators on pests and pollinators of crops. And third, perhaps most insidious, pesticides were accumulating in the tissues of organisms that were not their immediate target, poisoning birds and fish and mammals that fed on the insects or their predators. It was this last impact that prompted Rachel Carson to warn in her 1962 treatise *Silent Spring*—since recognized as one of the most influential books of the twentieth century—of a world in which wildlife was eerily absent. She wrote,

Over increasingly large areas of the United States, spring now comes unheralded by the return of the birds, and the early mornings are strangely silent where once they were filled with the beauty of bird song. This sudden silencing of the song of the birds, this obliteration of the color and beauty and interest they lend to our world has come about swiftly, insidiously, and unnoticed by those whose communities are as yet unaffected.

By 1972 the Environmental Protection Agency had banned DDT in the United States—the direct result of intense public pressure triggered by Carson's cautionary tale. Yet other insecticides remain in rampant use, and the World Health Organization now estimates that each year there are twenty-five million cases of pesticide poisoning and as many as twenty thousand unintentional deaths, primarily in developing countries. That is why there is an urgent need for a more benign form of insect management— the use of natural predators, parasites and pathogens to control insect pests. Just how benign such pest management can be was proven in a twenty-one-year-long Swiss study of organic farming published in 2002 in the journal *Science*. It showed that fields free of synthetic pesticides and fertilizers, though producing slightly lower yields, require a far lower input of energy. They also have healthier soil and a more abundant diversity of organisms, including three times as many earthworms and twice as many pest-consuming spiders and arthropods, as well as more beetles and wild plants.

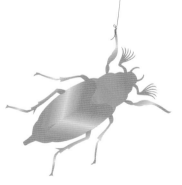

MELON APHID
Aphis gossypii

Small, frail, herbivorous, fecund: The aphid is the rabbit of the insect world. It is also the cow and the carrier pigeon, ants "farm" it for the honeydew it excretes from its anus and infectious viruses hitch a ride with it from plant to plant. Truly, the aphid is a versatile little beast, but most humans consider it a pest. Sucking sweet sap from thousands of plant species across the planet, aphids pierce cell walls with their needle-sharp proboscises, probing the plant's pipelines for the proteins and sugars they need to grow and reproduce. This one, the melon aphid or *Aphis gossypii*, is considered one of the most destructive in the United States, it feeds on the leaves of squash and cotton, strawberries, beans, beets and eggplants, turning them brown and wilted.

Aphids are voracious but defenseless, their soft little bodies are prime food for predators. They have, however, evolved two handy methods of self-protection. First, they hire security guards—ants that stroke their backs to "milk" their honeydew, driving away marauders in return. Honeydew is actually the by-product of meal that is 85 percent carbohydrate and 3 percent protein; to extract the protein, the aphids must suck a lot of sap. But the substance baffled many early naturalists. Pliny the Elder wrote, "Honeydew is either a certain sweat of the sky, or some unctuous gellie proceeding from the stars, or rather a liquid purged from the air when it purifyeth itself."

The aphid's other weapon is its extraordinary fertility. All through the summer, virgin females give birth to live young without the aid of sex. So prolific are they that one female aphid can produce as many as seven live offspring a day, prompting the eighteenth-century French scientist René-Antoine Réaumur to calculate that, if left to breed unchecked, the descendents of this one insect—nearly six billion of them—could march four abreast in military formation along the equator all around the globe. Only in autumn do females give birth to males, which, lacking mouths and living briefly, serve only to mate before they die. Then the females can lay eggs to last through winter.

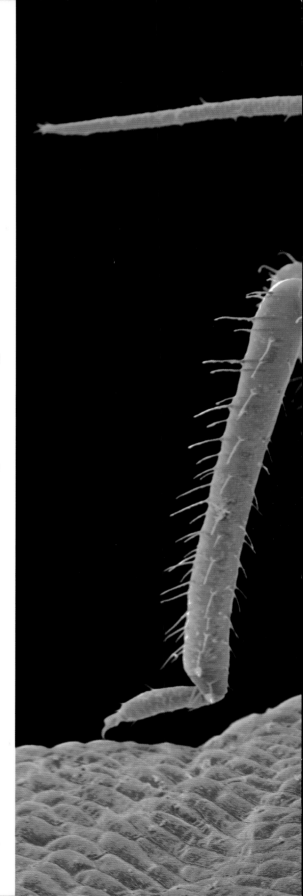

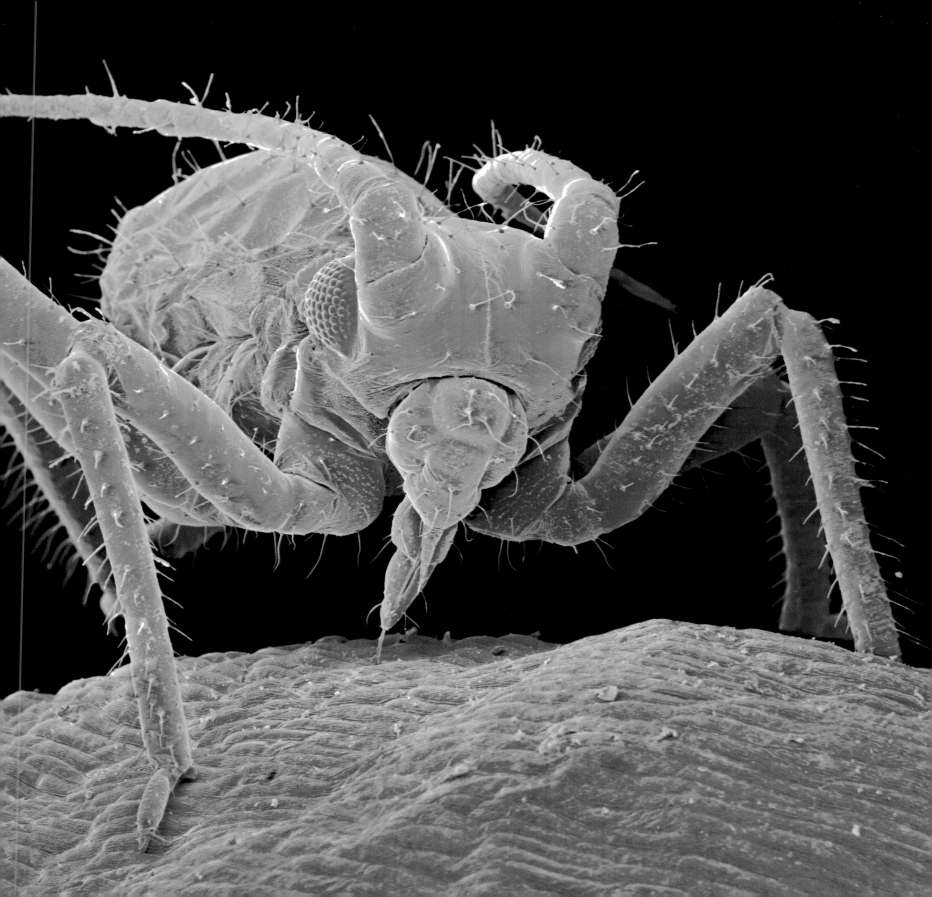

SEVEN-SPOTTED LADYBUG
Coccinella septempunctata

If you stand very quietly beside a feeding ladybug, you can hear it munching. The seven-spotted ladybug, or *Coccinella septempunctata*, caught here stuffing an aphid into its capacious maw, is a ravenous beast—it can consume several hundred aphids in one day. The ladybug stands on four legs and uses the front two to grab prey and jam it into its mouth. Dedicated in the Middle Ages to the Virgin Mary, "The beetle of Our Lady,"—known in Britain as a ladybird, and by French farmers as "the Cow of the Lord"—has long been deemed a harbinger of good fortune and fine weather. The seven-spotted ladybug is even said to cure toothache when crushed and crammed into a cavity.

The many different species of ladybug are important predators of crop pests such as aphids, mites and scale insects, and will even feed on the eggs of moths and potato beetles if other prey are scarce. In fact, one of the first successful large-scale experiments in biological control involved a species of ladybug, *Rodolia cardinalis*, or the vedalia beetle, imported in 1888 from

Australia to the United States to feed on the cottony cushion scale, *Icerya purchasi*. This destructive insect had killed hundreds of thousands of California citrus trees by sucking sap from their leaves, twigs, branches and trunks; yet within one year of the introduction of the vedalia beetle, the citrus industry was saved.

Business in ladybugs is still thriving. Every autumn millions of these insects hibernate in the California mountains; and just as regularly the pickers, or "buggers" show up to harvest them, shoveling them into sacks and selling them by the gallon to suppliers of beneficial insects. Companies like The Bug Factory, in Nanoose Bay, Canada, not only buy ladybugs but raise their own in insectaries—little gobblers like the mealybug-eating *Cryptolaemus*, as well as predatory mites and flies and the spined soldier bug, which paralyzes caterpillars with its small harpoon. Most of these predators are destined for zoos, citrus crops, greenhouses and butterfly gardens.

SEVEN-SPOTTED LADYBUG
LARVA Coccinella septempunctata

Yum. Raw aphid for lunch, chock-full of vitamins and sugary plant syrup. Succulent aphids for breakfast and dinner, too, and for brunch and afternoon tea. It's aphids all day for this ladybug larva, which will spend its entire three-to-four week juvenile life in an insatiable quest for plant pests to chomp on. Once known as an "aphis wolf," this carnivorous creature can hunt down hundreds of the little crawlers, roaming many yards in search of eggs as well as adults.

No wonder farmers and gardeners love ladybugs, since the aphids they eat are an enormous nuisance. Their incessant sap-siphoning shrivels plant leaves, shutting down photosynthesis and preventing the formation of fruit. Any fruit that does develop is often misshapen or shrunken. Because they coat stems and flowers in a sticky spread of honeydew, fueling the growth of a fungus called sooty mold, any produce that does form may be impossible to sell. (Though others take advantage of it, the "manna" that the biblical Israelites ate in the Sinai desert is often said to be

honeydew.) Aphids are also important vectors of plant viruses, over three hundred different species transmit them. Viruses cling to the aphid's mouthparts and are injected into new plants mechanically or mixed with saliva after circulating in the aphid's gut. The damage the viruses can inflict is colossal, whole fields can be destroyed by such pathogens as sugar beet yellow virus and tomato wilt virus.

Aphids have enemies, however—and not just ladybugs. Cold kills them. So do fungi. Birds feast on them. Humans douse them with suffocating oils and insecticides. And parasitic wasps lay their eggs inside them, turning their skin crusty and golden brown—a state known as a "mummy." When these carapaces appear on crops, the aphid population is likely to crash within a week.

CABBAGEWORM
Pieris rapae

This bristly beast is a great traveler: it followed in the footsteps of European colonists. Wherever they went and planted cabbages, one was sure to find *Pieris rapae*, the cabbageworm or cabbage white caterpillar, nestling in its leaves, chewing big holes in the foliage and depositing little pellets of excrement in its wake. Not a pleasant item to find in your soup. Or your salad. The cabbageworm has a fierce appetite for any plant containing mustard oil: Radishes, turnips, horseradish, watercress, cauliflower, cabbages, kale and kohlrabi. (Its Latin name is probably derived from the Greek word *rapavi*, or "radish.")

Most insects (and many small children) are repulsed by vegetables containing mustard oil, because it is chock-full of nasty-tasting sulfur-incorporating compounds called glucosinolates. These compounds have shown promise as natural alternatives to chemical insecticides, but cabbageworms are immune to their effects; for some strange reason, they find mustard oil delectable. They can be found crawling slowly over cabbages in most of the United States and Canada, chewing steadily until they are ready to spin silk cocoons, pupate and metamorphose into familiar pale white butterflies with black spots on their wings.

Cabbageworms can, however, be controlled. Beetles, flies and daddy longlegs (harvestmen) feed on them, parasitic wasps lay eggs in them, and viruses infect them. One insect, the paper wasp, evidently uses them as infant formula, ripping the caterpillars into bite-sized chunks and carting them home to their offspring. "Wasp larvae need meat to grow, and they need a lot of it," says Linda Rayor, who studies them at Cornell University. "Compared to a caterpillar, paper wasps are Einsteins, capable of learning and amazingly complex behavior. They hunt down caterpillars long distances from their nests; and if there is an outbreak of caterpillars, the wasps target them very effectively. They are singularly important biocontrol agents."

COMMON YELLOW JACKET
Vespula vulgaris

Watch out! Someone wants your sandwich. The common yellow jacket, *Vespula vulgaris*, seems to have an irresistible impulse to pilfer the picnic basket, especially if it contains sweet items such as chocolate or jam. Adult wasps such as this one feed primarily on nectar, honeydew and the juice from ripe fruits; they need energy, and their larvae, for whom they go out foraging, need flesh in order to grow. That meat is mainly of arthropod origin. One study published in 1968 documented in meticulous detail the prey captured by four colonies of ground-dwelling *V. vulgaris* at one locale in the Netherlands. The harvest included thirty different species of insect, mostly adult flies, as well as eight species of spider and many caterpillars. One wasp was even seen pulling a struggling fly from a spider web.

Wasps are voracious and tenacious. "When a wasp locates its prey, it normally pounces vigorously on the victim, frequently knocking it to the ground from the flower or wall on which the prey has been feeding or sunbathing," writes J. Philip Spradbery in his 1973 treatise *Wasps*. "The wasp kills by biting into the neck of the victim, often decapitating the prey within seconds." Such a propensity for insect flesh makes wasps ideal agents for biological control. In Canada, a species of *Vespula* has been shown to predate heavily upon the fall webworm, *Hyphantrea cunea*, a caterpillar that builds communal silk tents over the leaves of cherry trees, willows and ash. Others species of wasp—primarily *Polistes*, the paper wasps—attack economically significant pests such as cutworms and spring cankerworms, which chew the leaves off oaks, elms and maple trees. *Polistes* also target gypsy moth larvae, using their mandibles to carefully cut the defensive spines off the caterpillars before chewing them up.

The average human doesn't give a hoot about wasps' beneficial effects, though. Mild hysterics is the more typical response to a scavenging yellow jacket. Bad move, says Jim Carpenter, curator of entomology at the American Museum of Natural History and self-styled expert on wasp-induced "patio trauma." "If you start flailing your arms, they may sting you," he says. "If you just shared your picnic, it would be no problem." Carpenter, who has hunted wasps in fifty countries on three continents, believes that the beauty and sheer diversity of wasps are woefully under-appreciated. Such diversity was underlined during a 2003 "BioBlitz" of New York's Central Park to document every single species of plant, animal and fungus found within. On a four-hour trek through the park's bushes and undergrowth, Carpenter and his entourage found fifteen species of bee and five different species of wasp, including a European paper wasp and a fearsome queen yellow jacket out searching for a nesting site.

Coenosia humilis EATING A FRUIT FLY

It's a bug-eat-bug world out there. One day you're flying about minding your own business, looking for a moldy banana or other fermenting fruit to feed on, and the next thing you know some winged fiend has swooped down and nabbed you in midair, pierced your neck with its proboscis and sucked the life blood out of you. The fiend in this case is the tropical fly *Coenosia humilis*, and its hapless prey is the fruit fly *Drosophila melanogaster*, an insect with possibly the longest biography in the history of entomology.

C. humilis is a predatory fly released into greenhouses to gobble on pests such as whiteflies, leaf miners and black fungus gnats. It's an efficient eater, in one day each *C. humilis* can devour seven black fungus gnats, whose larvae cause tremendous damage by feeding on roots, stunting or killing young plants; they also spread fungal diseases such as *Pythium* and *Verticillium*. By contrast *Drosophila* is not a major pest except in the canned-tomato and dried-fruit industries; its relative the Mediterranean fruit fly is far more destructive, laying its eggs in peaches, pears, plums, guavas, kumquats and loquats, as well as several nuts. *Drosophila melanogaster* owes its renown instead to its utility as a model genetic organism. Since 1909, when Thomas Hunt Morgan first began studying it, scientists have bred it by the billion, dissected its chromosomes, and produced all manner of mutants, including one with legs growing out of its head. Finally, in 2000, researchers sequenced its entire genome, showing that it has just under 14,000 genes—about half of which it shares with humans.

Musca domestica
CAUGHT IN A FLYSWATTER

Thwack it with a flyswatter. It's the oldest and most obvious form of insect control, if not the most efficient. For the insect, it's the equivalent of being chased by a gigantic dodgem car driven by a deranged Goliath. Small wonder that it will bob and swoop to avoid the onslaught. But there was no escape for this common housefly, *Musca domestica;* it's been completely crumpled on the grid of this swatter, its wings mauled, its guts spilled, its legs mangled.

Brutal though it may sound, there are good reasons to go after houseflies. Breeding in dung, spreading dirt and disease as they vomit on food to dissolve and digest it, the housefly is more than mere nuisance. Victorian naturalist Sir John Lubbock called them "winged sponges spreading hither and thither to carry out the foul behests of contagion." The ubiquitous housefly, found at one time or another in every home in the world, has been accused of carrying more than twenty human illnesses, among them diarrheal diseases, typhoid, dysentery, cholera, parasitic worms and trachoma, a major cause of blindness. Unlike mosquitoes, which transmit disease in their saliva, the housefly need only brush its hairy body beside infectious germs in order to collect and spread them. One team of scientists discovered an average of 1.3 million bacteria clinging to each of the 414 flies they examined, picked up no doubt from carcasses and animal excrement. Such ordure is especially enticing to houseflies, who lay their eggs in it. It has been estimated that a half-ton pile of manure will after four days' exposure contain about 400,000 fly larvae, or 400 flies to the pound.

Crushed flies cause problems of their own. A buildup of bugs on airplane wings and helicopter rotors can seriously impede their operation. One study by Dutch scientists found that the power output of wind turbines can drop by 25 percent in high winds due to the accumulation of insect residue. Simply cleaning the blades, therefore, can avert a potentially catastrophic power failure.

MAY BUG
Melolontha melolontha

To nestle noiselessly in the soil, gnawing on roots and tubers, is all the May bug larva asks of life. But this one will never gnaw again, it has a fungus festering upon it. Although fungi can cause a variety of plant diseases—rusts, smuts, rots and wilts—they also attack plant enemies, particularly those that dwell in the earth. The May bug, also known as the common cockchafer, is one such crop foe. Emerging as adults during the warm spring evenings, the shiny inch-long reddish-brown bugs fly toward light and feed on the leaves of fruit and forest trees, particularly oaks, maples and sweet chestnuts. Then, when they are sated and sexually mature, they lay dozens of small, pearl-like eggs deep in the soil. The feeding begins soon after they hatch. For three years the white grubs graze underground, slicing grasses from their roots and furrowing holes in beets and turnips.

But the May bug, in Latin *Melolontha melolontha,* is itself attacked in turn. Mechanical cultivation kills the fragile larvae, and soil-dwelling fungi infiltrate their innards and rot them from within.

The green fungus in this photograph, *Metarhizium anisopliae,* infects some two hundred species of insects and was first used as a form of biocontrol against the wheat grain beetle way back in 1879. Fungal filaments called hyphae penetrate the insects via tiny pores called spiracles, the entryways into its network of ventilation tubes or tracheae. There the hyphae multiply, consuming the insects' entrails before breaking forth and releasing spores. So insidious is *Metarhizium* that biocontrol companies now mass-produce the spores and sell them. It's particularly effective against termites and ticks.

Not all fungi are insect enemies, however. Some that are pathogenic to plants hitchhike to new hosts on insects such as the fungus gnat. And leaf-cutting ants of Central and South America cultivate vast fungus gardens underground, growing their own food on piles of crushed leaf paste mixed with their own saliva.

Araneus diadematus
EATING A FLY

JOURNALIST: *Good evening, Mr. Spider, or rather, Mrs. Spider.*
SPIDER: [in a strident voice] *Are you edible?*
JOURNALIST: *Well, I think I am, but this is a matter that's never come up.*
SPIDER: *You know, we have quite a number of eyes, but we are very short-sighted, and we're hungry all the time. For us the world is divided into two parts: Things you can eat, and the rest.*
Primo Levi, "Five Intimate Interviews," from *The Mirror Maker*, 1986

"Things you can eat." Well, for a spider, that would be just about anything, all forms of insects, plant-feeding as well as predatory, and other spiders, including those of their own species. Of course the really big ones—some of the tarantulas of South America and the barking spiders of Australia—may kill frogs and lizards. The garden cross spider *Araneus diadematus*, pictured here, seems benign by comparison. It just injects a paralyzing poison into its insect prey that also liquefies its insides, enabling the spider to suck it dry and leave behind an empty, lifeless shell.

The spider's colossal appetite for insects and its cosmopolitan existence would seem to make it the ideal biocontrol agent. Spiders—which are not insects but eight-legged arthropods called arachnids—are found just about everywhere. Indeed, they are often the first animals to colonize recently erupted volcanoes, not by design but because they disperse themselves by ballooning with the wind across miles of open space on fine silk threads. Yet their voracity is also a liability, not only do spiders eat beneficial insects like ladybugs, but they are also cannibals, thus precluding the possibility of breeding them in large numbers.

Spiders can play an important role in controlling insect pests, however. Ecologist Ann Rypstra of Miami University in Ohio has found that stocking field rims in spring with old peach crates on which spiders can spin webs can significantly reduce the amount of soybean leaf damage. The mere presence of spiders or their silk seems to scare away pests: Japanese beetles, for example, will eat less of a leaf if a spider has ambled about on it. Researchers propose splicing spider silk genes into crops, or even incorporating their silk into insecticides, to reduce the frequency of insect attack.

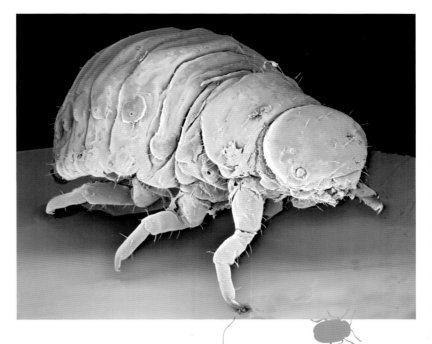

COLORADO POTATO BEETLE
LARVA Leptinotarsa decemlineata

Does this lumbering larva look like a weapon of mass destruction? Maybe not, to the uninitiated eye. According to a recently declassified U.S. military intelligence report, however, the Colorado potato beetle was once the focus of a failed German plan to target Britain with thousands of "bug-bombs." In 1942 a German spy communiqué from Britain reported the purported arrival there of an American airplane loaded with 15,000 potato beetles. Fearing an Allied scheme to harm their food supplies, the German authorities set up a Potato Beetle Defense Service, or *Kartoffelkäferabwehr-dienst*, which was charged with protecting German crops and preparing a counter-offensive. The plan was abandoned when nearly all of the insects vanished during an abortive field trial. Later, in 1950, the East German agriculture minister accused the United States of dropping beetles from aircraft flying over his country—a claim the Americans dismissed as propaganda.

Espionage and conspiracy theory aside, the Colorado potato beetle—*Leptinotarsa decemlineata*—is in fact an extremely destructive pest. Both the black-and-yellow-striped adults and the red, black-spotted larvae like this one feed on potato leaves and shoots, eating so insatiably that the plants often die. Once, however, the beetle was far more benign. When American colonists first encountered it in 1824 on the eastern slopes of the Rocky Mountains, it was just an insignificant feeder on a weed called buffalo bur. It was only when settlers began planting a new food—potatoes—that the beetles began to spread, traveling about eighty-five miles a year in pursuit of their favorite tubers. And not just this vegetable: the beetles can also subsist on tomatoes, eggplants, tobacco, peppers and petunias.

The Colorado potato beetle is a supreme example of an insect that has become resistant to nearly all classes of insecticide. But it is still susceptible to parasites and fungi, as well to *Bacillus thuringiensis*—a bacterium that produces an insecticidal toxin now incorporated into many genetically modified crops.

Araneus diadematus
EATING A FLY

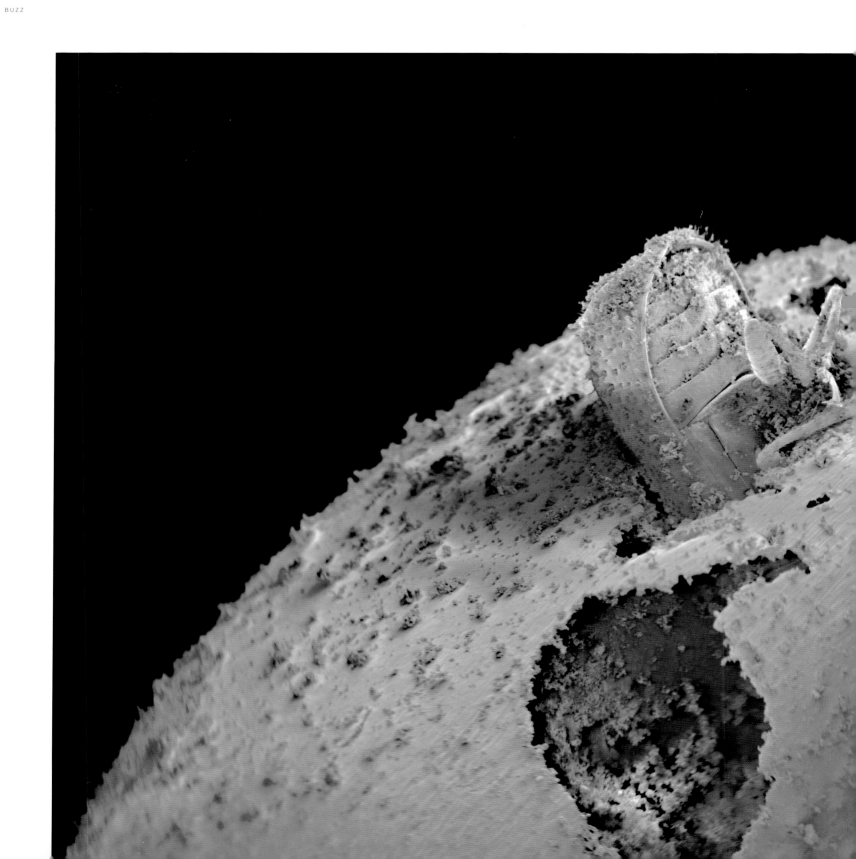

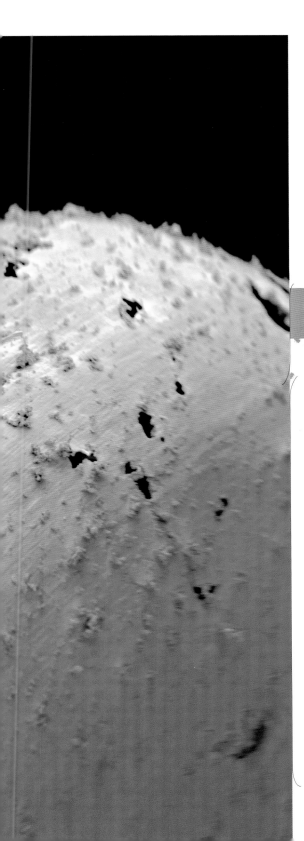

LARGER GRAIN BORER
Prostephanus truncatus

This is one bug for whom the label "boring" is a compliment. Boring is its forte. Burrowing deep into grains of corn, excavating little tunnels into which it lays its eggs, the larger grain borer, *Prostephanus truncatus*, is a digger supreme. This one with its butt sticking out of a morsel of maize has found itself a paradise. But the ecstasy is for itself alone: For the humans who grew the crop, it's an extreme nuisance. *P. truncatus* is a native of Mexico, where maize itself was first domesticated, and where the bug no doubt caused trouble enough. When it first appeared in Africa in the early 1980s it truly began to wreak havoc. In Tanzania, where farmers nicknamed it "dumuzi"—the destroyer—crop losses of 40 percent or higher were soon reported. In Benin, traditional methods of storing maize in structures called *awas* were rendered redundant—the larger grain borer can turn a corncob into dust within a few months.

What to do? Pesticides were the obvious answer, but *P. truncatus* is protected from most common insecticides that do not reach the inside of the cob where the grain borer burrows. As eventually became clear, it craves not only corn but also seeks refuge in wood. In Kenya it was found to subsist and reproduce quite comfortably on sixteen different species of tree, and it can also drill into wooden tools and the wooden frames of infested maize cribs. Thus spraying corn alone will not eliminate it. Instead, ecologists turned to its region of origin, and found in Costa Rica, its natural enemy: *Teretrius nigrescens*, a shiny black predatory beetle armed with sharp sickle-shaped jaws with which it can tear soft legless borer larvae to pieces. In early field tests in Togo, Kenya and Benin, the borer-feeding beetle was found to reduce corn crop losses by between 30 and 80 percent, though it now appears to be a somewhat less efficient biocontrol agent than anticipated.

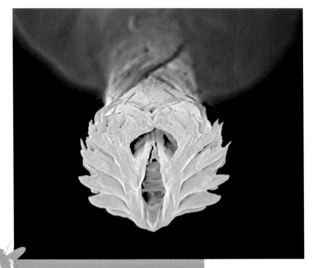

STABLE FLY
Stomoxys calcitrans

"The fly is a loathsome, pestilential, impudent, tiresome and restless insect," wrote Johann Sperling in his 1661 work *Zoologia physica*. "Flies sample almost everything and lick everything, but are particularly greedy for blood." Sperling didn't specify which fly he was referring to, but he could easily have been describing *Stomoxys calcitrans*, the stable fly. This insect could out-compete Count Dracula with its swordlike proboscis, which it uses to pierce the skin and suck the blood of horses, cows, hogs, dogs, cats, goats, rats and on occasion, humans. *S. calcitrans* needs blood to reproduce, though it can survive on nectar and pollen for about two weeks when on long-range dispersal flights.

The stable fly is a vicious pest. Swarms of these biting beasts can so torment cattle that they lose weight and yield less milk. In zoos they attack the ears of big cats, feeding voraciously until large hard-to-heal sores develop. Dogs' ears are another favorite target, as are the pads on bears' feet. Stable flies have also been shown to transmit diseases, including swamp fever, a viral disease of horses, as well as anthrax, brucellosis and bovine diarrhea virus. That the insect is so victorious an invader is probably due in part to its clever exploitation of the weather for long-distance transport. Jerry Hogsette, an entomologist with the U.S. Department of Agriculture, has shown that stable flies can detect an approaching weather system by the decrease in barometric pressure, which triggers flight and allows them to be swept up and carried miles away at high altitudes. This is probably how the stable fly, which originated in Africa, was able to follow the migrating herds on which it feeds.

Farmers are less fascinated by the flies' feats of flight. They just want to get rid of them. Alas, pesticides and repellents tend to be effective for a few hours only. Far better, says Hogsette, to rid stables of the flies' breeding grounds—hay and manure, spilled feed and wet, fermenting vegetation in which their larvae mature.

CRIME

WELCOME TO THE BODY BANQUET

O hideous little bat, the size of snot
With polyhedral eye and shabby clothes
To populate the stinking cat you walk
The promontory of the dead man's nose

Karl Shapiro, from "The Fly" (1942)

Know from where you came:
from a putrefying drop;
and whither you are going:
to a place of dust, worms and maggots.

Ethics of the Fathers
(Mishna Avot),
Chapter 3, Verse 1

A dead body is a banquet table to corpse-eating insects. First served are the *hors d'oeuvres*, fresh flesh scented with acids and gases that signal the onset of decay to swift-settling blowflies and house-flies. Then there is the entrée: muscles and fats so enticing to ham beetles, with a side-dish of fermenting proteins for the cheese skip-pers. Carrion beetles and mites pick at the leftovers. But dermestid beetles and clothes moths crave only dessert, a dish of desiccated skin and hair. For entertainment there is of course egg-laying and the imbibing of body fluids.

CHACUN À SON GOÛT, as the French say: Everyone to their taste. Or, as in this case, every bug to its taste. A feast of rotten flesh may sound disgusting, but to a coffin fly or a larder beetle it's a delicacy. And as gruesome as the body buffet may sound, the plain fact is that without insects the world's waste would have piled up to prodigious heights and buried us long ago. Insects and other decomposers such as bacteria and fungi, by consuming and digesting corpses, slowly turn them into molecules that are themselves the building blocks of new organisms: Birds and trees and bees and yes, new human beings. It's the eternally cycling afterlife.

The life that seethes on the dead is also of serious interest to forensic entomologists. These are scientists who can estimate the time and place of death by examining the insects that alight on a corpse. That's because insects visit a body in discrete waves for months or years after death if a corpse is left unburied or abandoned outside. Blowflies, the earliest arrivals, can see or smell a corpse within hours or even minutes of death and will rapidly begin laying eggs in orifices or open wounds; the maggots into which they hatch can feed on a body for weeks. After three to six months they are gone, but others have moved in—cheese skippers, carrion beetles, ham beetles and histerid beetles. When the body is dry and tough, it is the turn of dermestid beetles and clothes moths, which eat tendons, dried skin, ligaments and hair. After about a year empty pupal cases and insect excrement remain, but even these have their own gourmands—mealworms and spider beetles, which scavenge for the final remnants.

Forensic entomologists take advantage of this well-defined timeline. By examining adult insects, their eggs, larvae or pupae, they can determine how long insects have lived on a corpse. That, in turn, can help detectives estimate how many weeks or months have elapsed since death. Entomologists can also help determine if a body has been stored inside or moved a long distance, because many bugs breed only in particular places—just in the home, or solely in cities, or only in hot climates. By inspecting the body parts on which maggots feed, they can deduce whether death was natural or the result of a crime, since insects often choose blood-steeped wounds on which to lay eggs. With the aid of toxicologists, entomologists can even tell if a person was an addict or poisoned prior to death, by analyzing bugs for signs of drugs.

Insects, as expert witnesses, have helped solve hundreds of crimes. They have convinced juries to sentence drug dealers, murderers and even poachers to jail. They have helped unravel cases of rape and child abuse. Such entomological detective work goes back many centuries. One of the earliest and most famous of these cases took place in thirteenth century China, as documented by Sung Tz'u in his detective handbook *Hsi Yuan Chi Lu*, or *The Washing Away of Wrongs*. In it he cites the case of a man found stabbed and killed by the roadside of a small Chinese village.

No one would admit to the crime, so a local investigator ordered all the men in the area to lay their sickles on the ground, side by side. Attracted by invisible traces of blood, the flies flew in and settled upon only one sickle—that belonging to a neighbor who had lent the dead man money. His crime exposed, "the murderer knocked his head on the ground and confessed."

Flesh-eating bugs have also left their calling cards on those who died long ago. Red-legged ham beetles, dermestids and fly pupae have been found in the mummies of Egyptian kings and even on the animals embalmed alongside them. Perhaps it was the fear of these tiny tomb intruders that led to a notable spell against beetles in the Egyptian Book of the Dead:

"Begone from me, O Crooked-lips! I am Khum, Lord of Peshnu, who dispatches the words of the gods to Re, and I report affairs to their master!"

BLOWFLY
Lucilia

This iridescent blowfly may subsist in the cesspool of life, but it is perfectly put-together for the task it must do. Take the large eyes of this specimen, known in Latin as *Lucilia*. Its compound eyes, consisting of thousands of individual facets, are particularly well adapted to seeing red and bloody wounds on which to lay its eggs. The antennae, as well as the hairs on its body and holes on its legs, are sensory organs, fine-tuned to detect the odor of decomposition: Acetic and butyric acid, acetone, phenol and methyl disulfide, all chemicals that give a rotting body its distinctive stench. So sensitive is this insect that it can spot a corpse when flying more than 115 feet above it.

Face it, the blowfly is not an inspiring insect. Its bristly head and bulbous eyes, its probing proboscis and its filthy ways do not exactly charm. Still, it has its admirers. In 1890, the long-forgotten B. Thompson Lowne, "late president of the Quekett Microscopical Club" set out to produce a short treatise on the insect, and ended up writing a two-volume, meticulously illustrated work called *The Anatomy, Physiology, Morphology and Development of The Blow Fly*. In the course of more than one thousand pages, Lowne described every aspect of its life cycle, from egg to maggot to pupa to adult. Of particular interest was the blowfly's mouthparts, with a moplike sucking device at its end consisting of numerous hollow tubes through which the insect pumps digestive juices. In other words, it vomits all over its food, dribbling enzymes onto decomposing tissue to dissolve it. Then it sips up liquid flesh in solution.

In truth, though, adults are not big eaters of bodies. What they're really keen on consuming is old bread or cookies. To a blowfly, a dead body is just a chance to breed. For it is there that they can lay their eggs.

BLOWFLY LAYING EGGS
Lucilia

Blowflies can locate a body within minutes of death if the corpse is left outside. In warm weather the first visitor is likely to be *Lucilia*, which lays tiny, two-millimeter-long eggs in patches around such orifices as the nose, ears and eyes, and also on open wounds. The moist environment ensures that the eggs don't dry out. Just to be on the safe side, *Lucilia* lays lots of eggs—up to three hundred at any one time. She does this up to ten times in her short life of just a few weeks.

In the realm of forensics, eggs can play an important role. Although they may take up to twenty-four hours to hatch, their presence, and the absence of any hatched maggots, suggests that death has occurred only recently. Gail Anderson, a forensic entomologist at Simon Fraser University in British Columbia, Canada, was able to help solve a poaching case by pinpointing the time of death of twin bear cubs shot and gutted for their gall bladders, a prized ingredient in some Asian medicines. Anderson found fresh blowfly eggs on the bodies of the bears, which were discovered in a Winnipeg garbage dump. "We watched the eggs until they hatched, so that we could count backwards and work out what time they had been laid," she says. That enabled her to narrow down the date of death to an evening on which the suspects in the case had been seen loitering around the dump. The defendants were sentenced to three months in jail.

The blowfly has inspired its own strange genre of poetry. In his 1961 poem "The Fly," Czech poet Miroslav Holub makes a pair of these insects the main protagonists of the fourteenth-century battle of Crécy, as they mate and cavort amidst the shouts, gasps and groans of the soldiers.

When silence settled
and only the whisper of decay
softly circled the bodies

and only
a few arms and legs
still twitched jerkily under the trees,

she began to lay her eggs
on the single eye
of Johann Uhr,
the Royal Armourer.

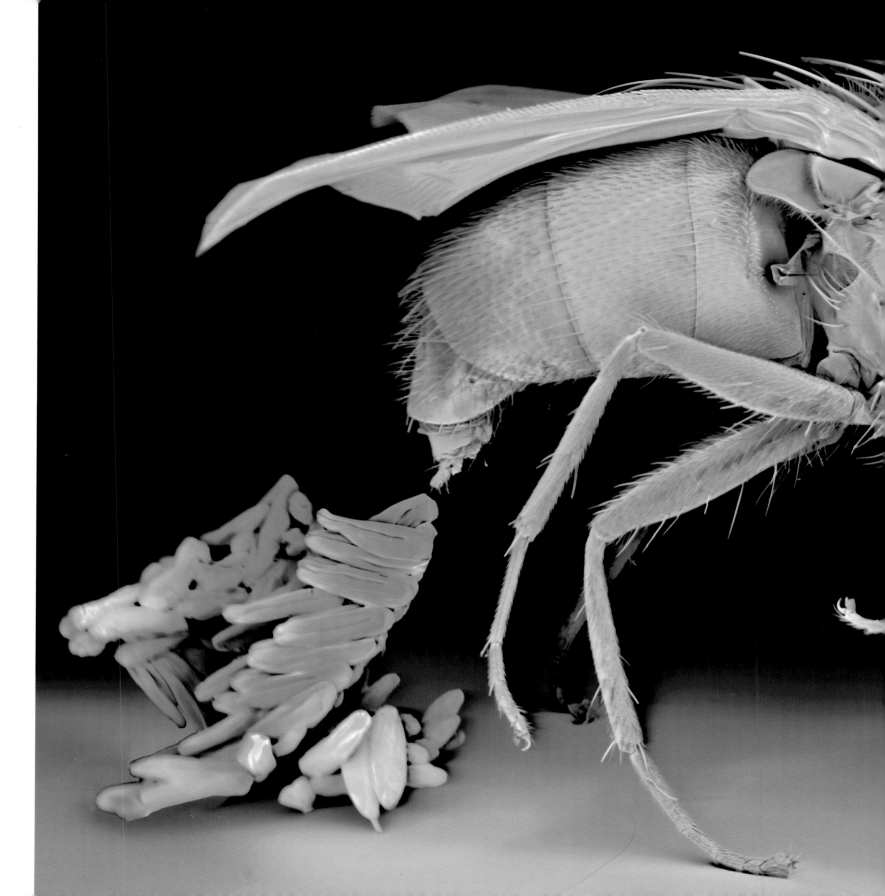

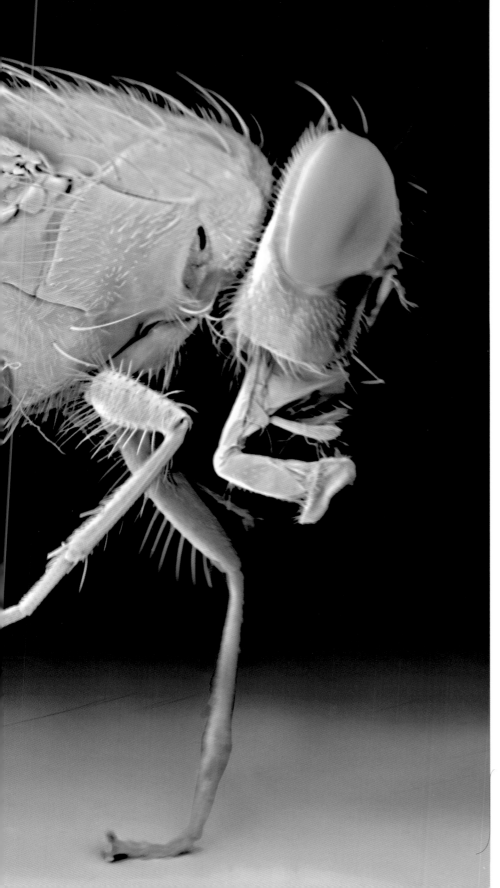

BLOWFLY LAYING EGGS

Lucilia

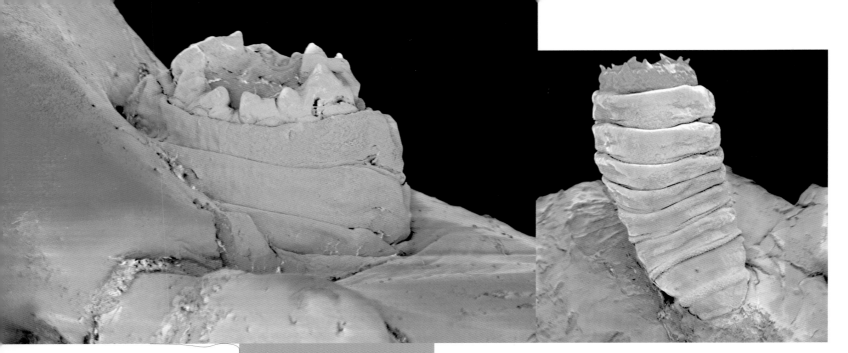

MAGGOT MUNCHING ON LIVER
Calliphora vicina

Let the great feast begin. This is a maggot of the blowfly *Calliphora vicina*, seen here burrowing into a small lump of liver. This little beastie has two tiny hooks with which it scrapes away at minuscule morsels of meat, exuding enzymes from its mouth that can digest fats and collagen, a protein found in skin, tendons and cartilage. Though it is deeply immersed in its meal, it has no trouble obtaining oxygen, little breathing holes arranged around its anus do that job with ease.

Calliphora maggots or larvae are rapid developers—they can go from egg to pupa within one to two weeks. The hotter it is, the faster they grow. Forensic entomologists can estimate the time of death by taking note of the outside temperature and the size of the maggots. They can also determine the nature of death by examining the entry points where maggots cluster. Blowflies prefer to lay their eggs in damp spots such as the mouth or eyes, avoiding dry skin unless it is injured. So maggots found elsewhere—in hands or arms, for instance—could indicate that the victim

tried and failed to fend off an attacker. Larvae can even reveal if a person was poisoned or drugged. Mercury, heroin, cocaine and the insecticide malathion have all been traced in maggots. Some drugs can even delay or speed up the growth of these insects. For example, high doses of cocaine can accelerate the rate at which certain sarcophagids, or flesh flies, develop.

M. Lee Goff, an entomologist at Chaminade University of Honolulu, was able to shed light on a mysterious death by examining some extra-large blowfly larvae found on the shirtless body of a woman found stabbed in a wood outside Spokane, Washington. From experiments in his lab on larvae that had fed on the livers of cocaine-dosed rabbits, he had found that such

maggots are hyperactive, feed more rapidly, and grow far faster. The blowfly larvae found on the stab victim were so big they seemed to be three weeks old, and yet other insects on the body suggested she had been dead just a few days. It turned out that the mega-maggots had been feeding around the woman's nose—right in the place where, shortly before death, she had been snorting cocaine.

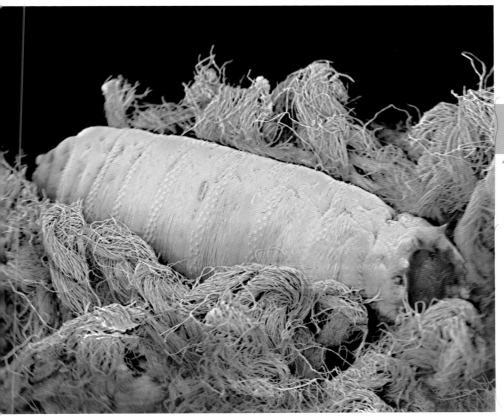

Calliphora
PUPA IN CARPET

"A pupa is like an M&M to a bird. The bird can go and pick up one pupa after another; they cannot crawl away," says Mark Benecke, a forensic entomologist based in the German city of Cologne. "As a pupa, you don't want to be seen." So when *Calliphora* maggots are full-grown—eighteen to twenty-four days after hatching—they drop off a body and creep away in search of a dark place in which to pupate. An unobtrusive spot is best—under a couch, beneath a book or tucked deep in a thick rug or below it. This one sitting nestled in a carpet is probably in the early stages of pupation, the torpid semiquiescent state in which the insect develops into an adult.

These days, forensic entomologists can do even more than merely use a maggot or a pupa as a guide to the time of death. Now they can actually analyze its final meal by identifying DNA lodged in its gut. These analyses, developed in the past few years, can be crucial in cases where the larvae remain but the body is gone. Such a crime was committed in 1989 in southern Italy when the mafia whisked away the body of a murdered man left in the cellar of an isolated farmhouse after an informant had notified the police that it was there. All that could be found in the cellar were large numbers of blowfly maggots, but no other biological evidence. Lacking the technology to detect human DNA in the maggot tissues, the police were unable to identify the body from the larvae left behind.

In future cases, however, they might be able to do so. After dissecting blowfly maggots fed on a human liver removed from a transplant recipient, scientists at the University of Alabama found human DNA amidst the insects' gut contents—DNA that matched that of the organ's former owner. Thus the technique could one day provide an indubitable link between the insects and the flesh upon which they once fed.

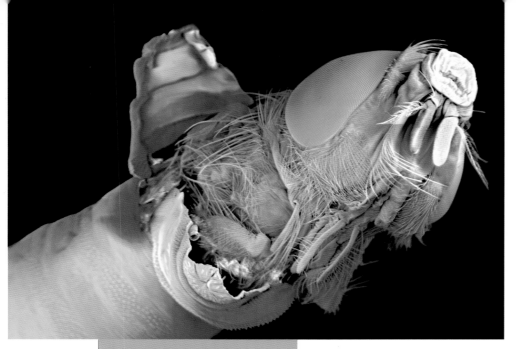

BLOWFLY HATCHING
Calliphora vicina

Here's a face only a blowfly biographer could love. Although B. Thompson Lowne lived long before the invention of the electron microscope, he would no doubt have waxed lyrical at this image of an adult *Calliphora vicina* emerging from its pupal case. Did he not devote a full fifty-four illustrated pages in his 1890 magnum opus *The Blow Fly* to its day-by-day development inside the pupa: The growth of its legs, the formation of its antennae, the spread of its wings? And was he not the first (and almost certainly the last) to weigh the blowfly brain, finding it to be one four-hundredth the mass of its body? Because even a blowfly has a brain, albeit a primitive one. As Lowne noted, a decapitated fly will for some hours clean dust or water off its wings or abdomen "by the same acts as

the entire insect," apparently because the nerves remaining in the rest of its body are autonomous enough to continue controlling its movements.

The emergence of a corpse-inhabiting insect from its pupa can be a good guide to when a crime occurred. Finnish forensic entomologist Pekka Nuorteva helped solve one such crime committed in the city of Helsinki in 1972. A man had dumped a blood-stained shirt, in a bag, in an outdoor garbage bin. The shirt was covered in fly larvae and some pupae of *Muscina*

stabulans, or false stable fly, which favor toilets and orchards and feed on rotting matter. When Nuorteva incubated the larvae in his lab, he found that two batches of *Muscina* eggs had been laid: one lot shortly after a crime had been committed, and the second when the shirt had been discarded. He knew this because two waves of adults emerged—the second twenty-eight days after the shirt was tossed into the trash. He could therefore calculate when the first batch of false stable fly eggs had been laid—on a date that coincided with that of a murder in the house from which the shirt-dumping man had emerged.

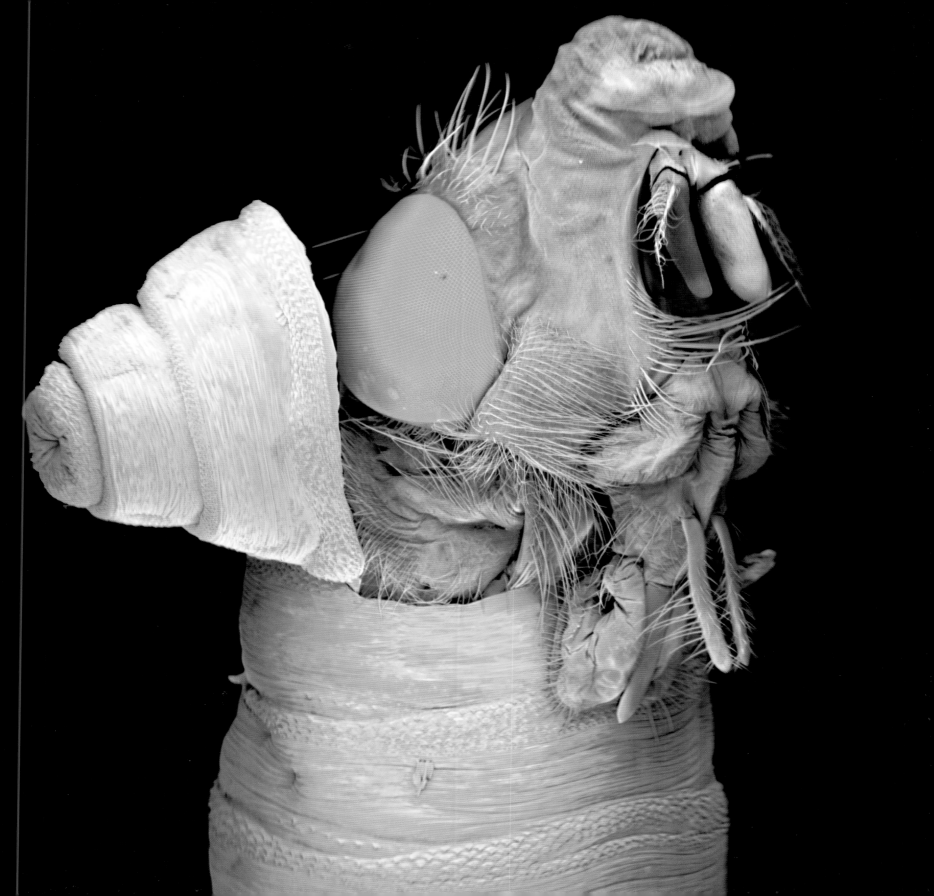

RED-SHOULDERED HAM
BEETLE Necrobia ruficollis

The ham beetles arrive two to four months after a death, when a body has begun to dry out. These insects are partial to dried or smoked meats, but they will also happily chew on cheese, herring, dried egg yolks, salted fish, palm nut kernels and dried coconuts—any food, in fact, that's rich in fat and protein. Before the advent of refrigeration they were a serious problem in storerooms, and are still found infesting pet shops and ports. Egyptian tombs are another favorite spot. The red-legged ham beetle, *Necrobia rufipes*, was found infesting the mummy of Ramses II, who died around 1235 B.C.E.

Ham beetles are truly not fussy about what they will taste. In a pinch, they will prey on the larvae of blowflies or cheese skippers, or even their own little eggs. And these cannibals can produce a lot of offspring. One adult female can lay up to twenty-eight eggs a day, or as many as three thousand eggs over her fourteen-month life. So they're not uncommon in corpses, favoring flesh with a texture resembling old leather. This one was found running around on the body of a half-buried dog in a park in Cologne. Because the adults are active in summer, their presence can signal the season death took place. When winter comes the larvae lie in wait.

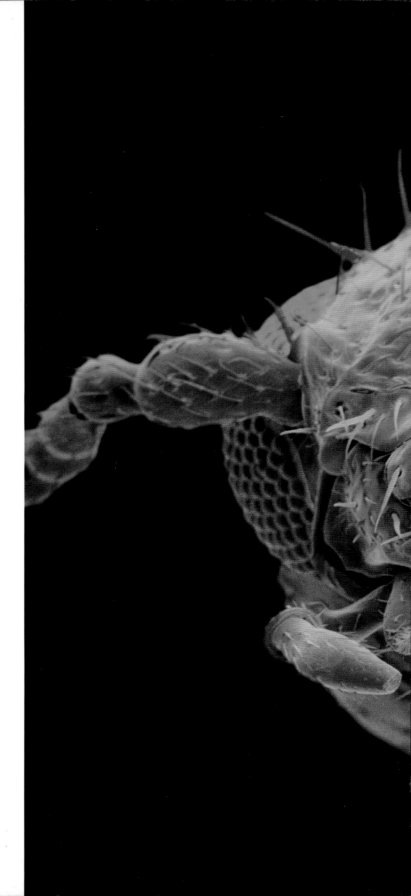

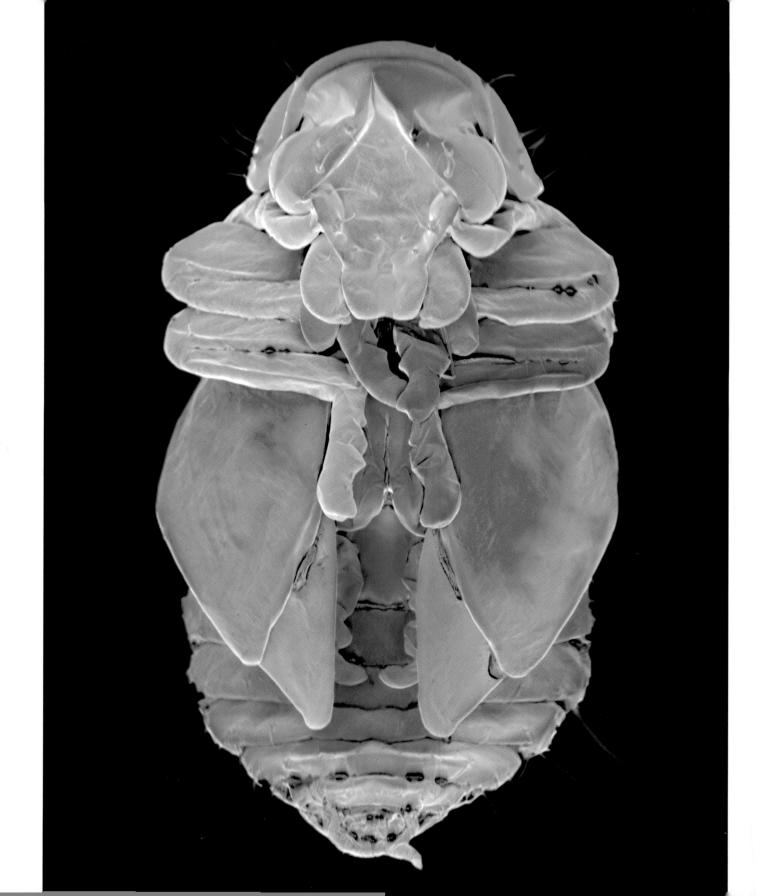

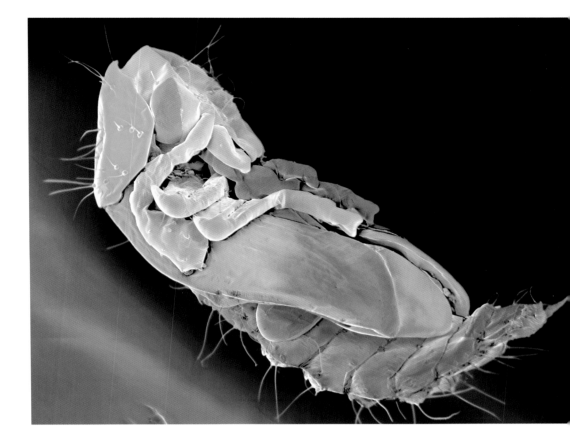

Necrobia
LARVA

Sometimes *Necrobia* larvae can also pop up on the witness stand. M. Lee Goff, a forensic entomologist at the Chaminade University of Honolulu, cites a case in which these beetles helped certify the date of death of a woman whose body was found buried in a cardboard box in a shallow grave on the island of Oahu. According to the police, her boyfriend John Miranda—who had been killed about two months earlier in a police shoot-out after taking a coworker hostage—had boasted of murdering her. But did she die before or after he did? If it was earlier, then it seemed likely that Miranda was her murderer. But if it was afterward, then police would need to seek another suspect.

When Goff examined the decaying body, he found a whole menagerie of bugs and worms and mites. There were millipedes and earthworms, muscid flies, rove beetles, hister beetles and larvae of the black soldier fly. There were also larvae of the red-legged ham beetle, *Necrobia rufipes*. By combining climate data with the information gleaned from this collection of invertebrates, Goff was able to determine that the woman had perished at least fifty-six days earlier—two days before Miranda had been shot. The prime suspect, therefore, was already dead.

Necrobia spends two-thirds of its life as a larva. When it's time to pupate, it seeks a dark spot, creeping away from the greasy foods in which it has grown. Then it begins to secrete a frothy goop from its mouth, spinning a silk cocoon in the crevice in which it is hidden.

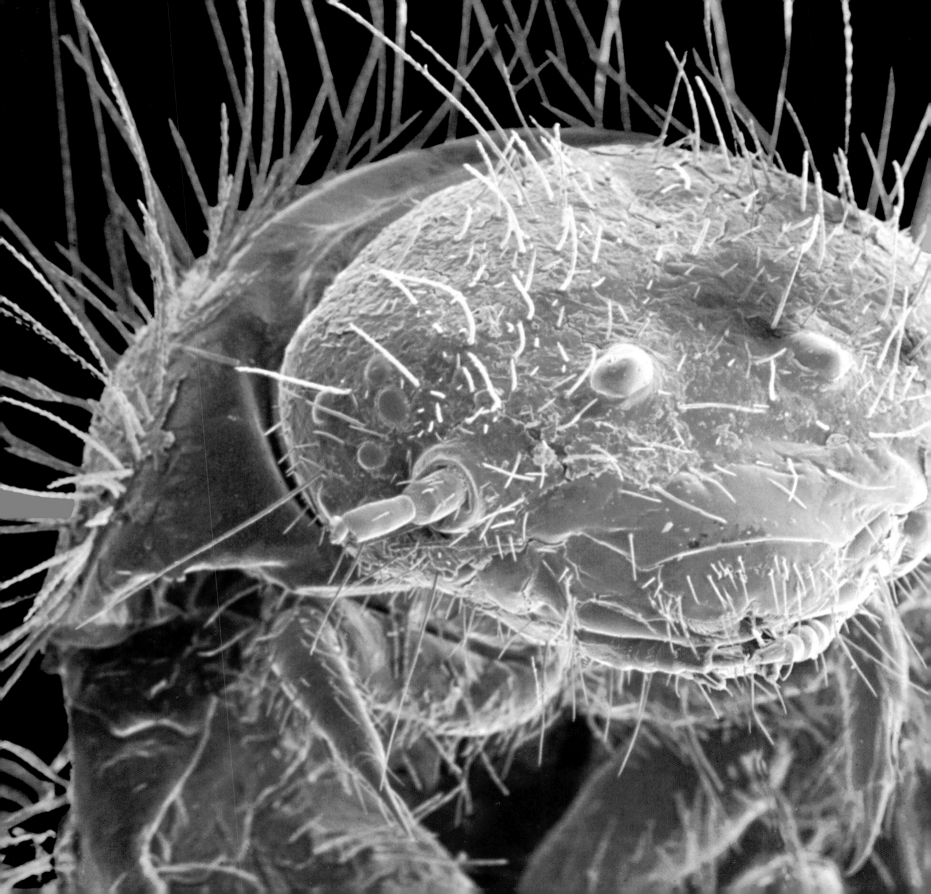

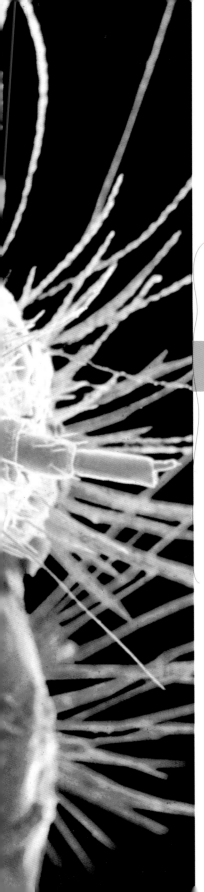

DERMESTID BEETLE LARVA
Dermestes lardarius

This fuzzy little animal favors furry things—hair, skin, feathers, a teddy bear, perhaps, as a treat, stuffed museum specimens, and also tobacco, pet foods, cheese, meat and beeswax. *Dermestes lardarius*, the larder or dermestid beetle, is a pest. When larvae like this one are looking for a protected crevice in which to pupate, they can even drill through timber, lead and tin.

Dermestid beetles are late arrivals at the body banquet. Both adults and larvae can clean desiccated tissue off a corpse, leaving dry bones behind. Natural history museums often enlist colonies of a related species, *Dermestes maculatus*, the hide beetle, to chew the muscle off small mammal skeletons. But usually these insects aren't so welcome. In 1981 curators at Britain's Bristol Museum unwrapped a three-thousand-year-old mummy of an Egyptian priest named Horemkenesi from the temple of Karnak and found that brown dermestid beetles had long ago bored tiny galleries into his arms, legs, feet and neck.

Larder beetles can also be found on more modern mummies. Forensic entomologist Mark Benecke found hundreds of them infesting the body of a man found slumped dead next to a radiator in his apartment. Hot air from the heater had dried his body very rapidly, giving no chance for blowflies to infest it. Instead dermestid beetles had colonized his mummified remains. "They took over the body," he says. "The eye sockets were filled with dermestid beetle feces, which you never find, because usually the eyes are eaten up by blowfly maggots. The body was nearly skeletonized. This is what the dermestids like, totally dried out tissue."

Dermestes
PUPAL CASE IN HAIR

"The sheer number of insects outnumbers any other entity of life," says forensic entomologist Mark Benecke. "We're guests in the world of insects." Sometimes we're also the hosts. This empty pupal case was discarded by a dermestid beetle in the overgrown hair of a half-dried corpse. Benecke retrieved it from the head of an alcoholic man several months after he had died alone in his apartment not far from his front door. Air seeping under the door had partially dehydrated the cadaver, and dermestid beetles already inhabiting the man's home made his body their new base. "There was already lots of dried-out matter in his apartment—a lot of open tins, bottles, jars filled with stuff, teabags, coffee grounds, lots of bags," says Benecke. "So the dermestids were already there."

In the open, dermestid beetles usually arrive on a body about two months after death. Therefore their presence can also indicate the so-called post-mortem interval. In his book *Maggots, Murder, and Men*, the late forensic entomologist Dr. Zakaria Erzinçlioğlu, a.k.a. "Dr. Zak," recalled a case in which the British police had asked him to estimate the date of death of a fifteen-year-old girl who had allegedly been murdered by a schoolboy acquaintance. Her body had been found in late July beside a railroad, covered in debris and populated by a diverse collection of insects, including large numbers of cheese skipper maggots. These insects, so-called because of their fondness for *fromage*, escape predators by hooking their front to their back ends and flinging themselves into the air. On the body Dr. Zak also found numerous dermestid grubs, which led him to conclude that the girl had died in mid-May—a date later corroborated by police investigations.

DIPTERAN FLY SLAMS INTO WINDSHIELD

Crash! This little two-winged fly had the misfortune to smash into a moving car windshield. While some would scrape it off with a muttered "yuck," others look a little closer, folk like Mark Hostetler, author of *That Gunk on Your Car*, the definitive guide to the insect splotch on your automobile. Hostetler, a wildlife biologist at the University of Florida in Gainesville, likes to hang out in bus stations, examining the fauna that fly into vehicles. Flat bus windshields are the best sites for finding splattered bugs, says Hostetler. "The flatter the windshield, the more likely they are to stick, body parts and all," he says. "On most passenger vehicles, they hit and ricochet up over the top, just leaving the residue."

Hostetler, who may be the world's sole expert on pulverized insects, estimates that millions of bugs meet their end every month by careening into windshields or other areas of auto anatomy. Moths are prime victims, because they are attracted to the lights on the highway, but mosquitoes and midges are frequent fatalities, too. One can learn a lot by probing into dead bug pulp. "You can tell the sex of the insect sometimes by the splat alone," explains Hostetler. "In mosquitoes, most flies, midges, it's the female that bites. So if you have a splat with a touch of red in it, it might be the blood meal of the female. She needs blood for the eggs to mature."

Crushed bugs can also contribute to the solving of crimes. Certain species of insect are found only in specific geographical regions, so identifying a particular pest stuck to a suspect's car can be a clue to the places to which the person has driven. Best of all, from a bug detective's point of view, are the insects that can become trapped into the treads of a tire—site-specific jumpers and crawlers like grasshoppers, cockroaches and especially ants. "In the air, you can always propose that an insect can fly over long distances, and the wind can also blow an insect quite far away," explains Mark Benecke. "But with tires, you can prove direct contact with the soil."

insects
as pets
and
performers

And here 'The Most
Intelligent Fleas', trained
reined, bridled, and bitted, minutely cavorted in their
glass corral.

Dylan Thomas
from "Holiday Memory," 1954

Sir John Lubbock, the first Lord Avebury (1834–1913), once kept a pet ant alive for nearly fifteen years. A member of the British parliament and author of *Ants, Bees, and Wasps: A Record of Observations on the Habits of the Social Hymenoptera* (1882), Sir John was one of those keen Victorian naturalists with the time, money and energy to dabble in many different branches of science, gathering specimens and artifacts from all over the globe. Among his near-contemporaries was the eccentric Sir Lionel Walter Rothschild, who once drove a zebra-harnessed carriage onto the forecourt of Buckingham Palace, and who bequeathed his collection of two million butterflies and moths to the British Museum upon his death in 1937. The Victorians were such fanatical butterfly hunters that they sent emissaries to far-off tropical forests in search of exotic species; though in truth they were more likely to stick pins in their hard-won prizes than maintain them as pets.

These days, the art of butterfly collecting is a less-fashionable one, in part due to the rarity of such dazzling quarry; many species of Lepidoptera have been driven extinct by habitat destruction and pollution. And yet many people still retain the old need to nurture insects. The Chinese, for example, have for thousands of years kept captive crickets, cicadas and katydids in elaborate bamboo cages, delighting in their songs. Although insect pets are not exactly affectionate, they do inspire their own odd breed of followers, folk who post stories on the Internet of their stick insects, or "pretty hearty 'lil buglets" climbing over the heads of oblivious house guests. Stick insects, rhino beetles, mantids, fruit beetles, ants and that fat brown beast, the Madagascar Giant Hissing Cockroach, can all be easily bred at home, in plastic containers or aquariums.

There are those for whom such insects are more than pets, though; they are performers. Call it strange, but some people would shun the most elastic of human acrobats in favor of a night at the flea circus, watching these tiny artistes kick footballs, twirl like ballerinas, pull chariots or turn carousels. Such enthusiasm seems tame, though, compared with that of a possibly apocryphal German king cited by the poet and playwright Goethe. This king had a favorite flea that he treated as his son, clothed in a robe of velvet, and upon which he bestowed the rank of chancellor. And though the queen and all her courtiers were itching from their bites, no one was allowed to harm the regal flea—or even be seen scratching.

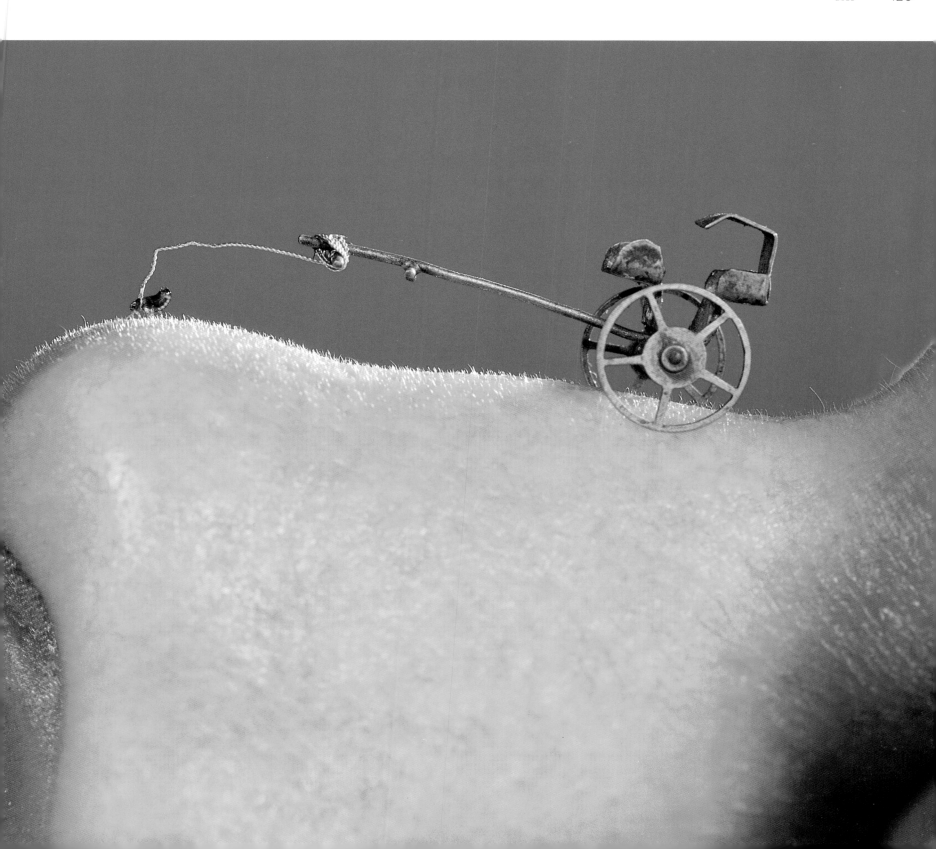

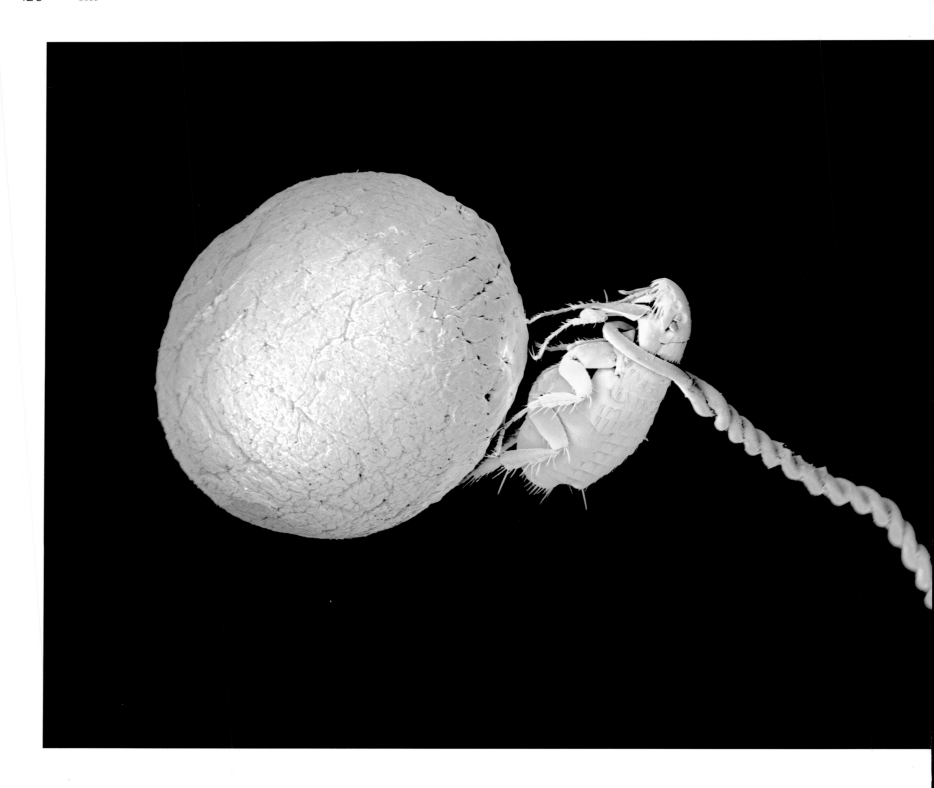

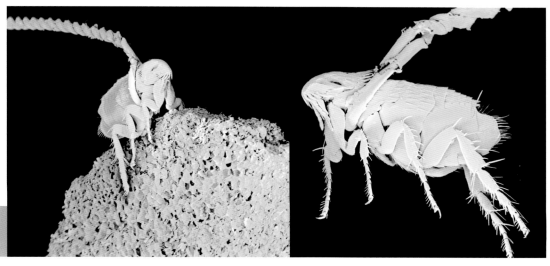

FLEA CIRCUS

A flea circus must certainly count as one of the most curious forms of performance art. Though its origins are obscure, it may be that odd brand of English eccentricity that first inspired such a display of insect dexterity and daring. Sixteenth-century writer Thomas Moufet—the possible father of that famous arachnophobic female, Little Miss Muffet—cites "Mark, an Englishman" as the one who first fastened a chain of gold around a flea, with which apparatus this insect "did draw a Coach of Gold that was every way perfect, and that very lightly; which much sets forth the Artists skill, and the Fleas strength."

Strength is the significant word here. One flea the size of a grain of sand can kick a ball thirty times its weight. It can jump more than thirty centimeters high and three times as far—the equivalent, in human terms, of an adult man vaulting from

London's Westminster Bridge to the top of Big Ben. Fleas owe their incredible leaping power to two tiny spheres of elastic protein, called resilin, located just above their hind legs. By compressing and then releasing the energy in the resilin balls, the flea is able to catapult itself through the air, lifting off at 140 times the force of gravity— more than 20 times that of the space shuttle.

The real trick in training fleas, though, is to persuade them not to jump at all, but instead to pull carriages, turn carousels, sword fight or dance a delicate ballet. Though much of this art remains a closely guarded secret—flea circus proprietors, who historically prefer the title "professor," tend to keep their techniques to themselves—some general principles are known. First, the fleas are enclosed in a bottle or a box sealed with a cork. Because they are sensitive to light, they tend to sit at the bottom of the bottle—until the cork is replaced with a glass top. Those that jump

and hit the glass habituate to its height, which is gradually lowered by decreasing the size of the container. Finally, they cease leaping and are now ready for the spotlight. Some remain jumpers, these are the soccer players, which shoot a ball into a miniature goal by bounding away from it. To thwart any attempt to escape, the proprietor carefully threads each flea's head through a tiny copper wire loop, then squeezes the loop slightly to tighten the harness.

Alas, flea circuses are not exactly in fashion these days. One reason is, ironically, the scarcity of the artistes. *Pulex irritans*, the human flea most favored as a

performer, has been hounded out of its chosen haunts by twenty-first-century hygiene. Nevertheless, a few die-hard humans remain dedicated to the art. One is Hans Mathes, who runs Europe's last remaining flea circus each year at the Munich Oktoberfest, and whose fleas, shown here, feed on blood from his own arm between performances. Another is "Professor" A. G. Gertsacov, whose Acme Miniature Circus, "starring Midge and Madge, Trained Fleas Performing Spectacular Circus Stunts As Seen Before (and on top of) the Crowned Heads of Europe," can purportedly still be found—if you peer very closely—touring some *very* small stages around America.

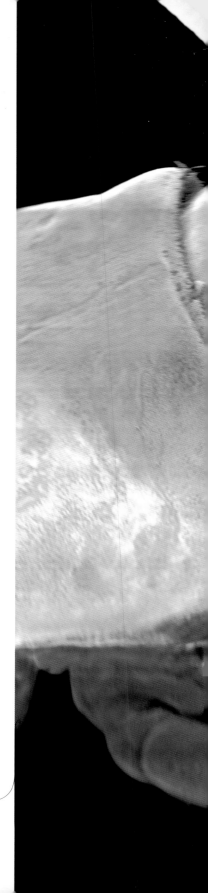

CRICKETS FIGHTING
Gryllus bimaculatus

CRICKETS FIGHTING
Gryllus bimaculatus

Move over Muhammad Ali, make way for the heavyweights of the insect kingdom. Crickets are fighters of fierce tenacity, a fact that fascinated the Chinese and fueled a spectator sport that stretches back to the Sung Dynasty (960 to 1278 c.e.). One so-called "Cricket Minister" of the period, Jia Shi-Dao, was so obsessed by the cricket-fighting craze that he wrote an entire book on the philosophy, literature and science of the sport. His bible of cricket lore is still consulted by cricket-fighting fans in China, where the cult retains a strong foothold. There are fighting clubs and societies dedicated to the sport, and in the autumn—the wrestling season before the insects die in winter—there are hundreds of crickets on sale in the Beijing bird and animal market. Buyers select champions for their size, speed, and strength of mouthparts, often betting huge sums of money on the outcome of matches.

It isn't only gambling enthusiasts who are enthralled by the tussles of crickets in combat. Scientists, too, study them for insights into aggression and conflict resolution. It seems that the course of cricket combat follows a sharply delineated sequence of advance and retreat that is seen throughout the animal kingdom. First, the contestants—usually male—fence with their antennae; then, one by one or both together, they spread their mandibles and show them off. If neither retreats, as can happen at any stage of the fight, they will interlock their mandibles as seen here, just as rams do with their horns. Finally they wrestle, pushing and tugging on one another, biting each other's body parts, struggling for dominance until one of them submits. The winner does a victory song and dance, while his defeated rival loses the will to fight for up to a day. Rarely, if ever, do they fight to the death.

"This stylized way of fighting, with lots of show and shouting, are the same kinds of things you see in conflicts between human tribal groups," says neurobiologist Paul Stevenson of the University of Leipzig in Germany, who has investigated a trick well known to Chinese cricket gamblers. The trainers know that if they shake their little wrestlers and toss them in the air, the loser will immediately regain the will to fight—and will be more likely to win the next round. After placing them in a wind tunnel and forcing them to fly, Stevenson and his colleague Hans Hofmann found that defeated crickets that flew even for a few seconds would challenge former opponents and wrestle with renewed vigor. Evidently, the act of flight triggers the release of a chemical that boosts aggression—and for good reason. Crickets, like any animal, fight to gain or defend resources—shelter, food, a mate. Any cricket that flies away after losing its territory would be fit to fight and win a new one when it lands.

MADAGASCAR GIANT HISSING COCKROACH

Gromphadorhina portentosa

OK, so it won't run to greet you, be your best friend or gaze at you with huge, limpid, loving eyes. But neither will it chew your slippers to shreds, slobber all over your nervous aunt or infuse the room with a foul odor. Many children consider these large, chocolate-brown, wingless roaches the ideal pets. They don't bite. They don't fly. They don't bark. They don't spread diseases, and their excreta exude no noxious smells. Perhaps pet owners keep *Gromphadorhina portentosa* for bragging rights, as it is the only insect to make a hissing sound, which it does by forcing air out of breathing holes on its abdomen, called spiracles, with the aid of small internal sacs that squeeze the air like bellows. At ninety decibels, it can be heard up to four meters away.

Native to the Madagascan rain forest floor, where they live among the leaf litter and feed on fallen fruit, these three-inch-long nocturnal roaches can be easily cared for in a warm, humid aquarium, with a climate mimicking that of their original home. As long as they are given a dark shelter in which to hide by day, and a steady diet of dog biscuits, celery, lettuce and carrots, they can live as long as five years. That's plenty of time to observe their life cycle, which is quite fascinating. Adult males are territorial, defending a harem of females against subordinate interlopers by strutting, or stilting, on their toes, by thrashing their abdomens or lunging with their entire body. Unlike females, which hiss only in alarm, the males have a whole repertoire of hisses: a combat hiss for fighting off rivals, two types of courting hiss, a mating hiss, and an alarm hiss to startle predators. When it comes to courting, though, the roaches are pure gentleness. Males and females mutually stroke each other with their antennae, hissing softly before mating. The female gives birth to live nymphs that develop, internally, in a purselike capsule called an ootheca that she first lays, then retracts, into a special cavity in her abdomen.

Madagascar roaches even have their own pets, spittle-eating mites. In return for a steady diet of roach saliva—which tends to accumulate in between the insect's legs—the mites fight off parasitic raiders. The relationship is of mutual benefit to both, the mites remain on the roach for all of its life and drink the water vapor that emerges from its spiracles.

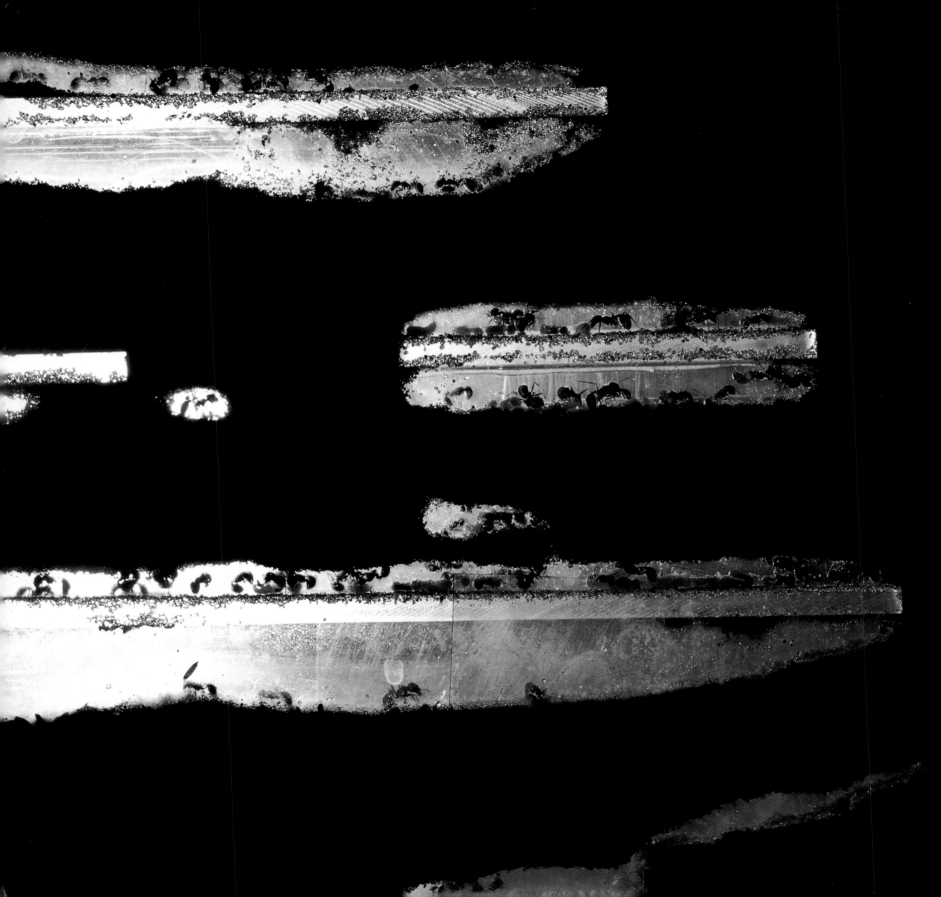

PHOTOGRAPHER'S NOTE

Bugs are very photogenic—especially when photographed with a scanning electron microscope. A bulky machine composed of vacuum pumps, an electron beam and a computer, the SEM scans microscopic objects and produces images with a greater depth of focus than conventional light microscopes or more standard photographic setups. Images produced by the SEM are black-and-white, so it is important to note that the microscopic photography in this book has been computer colorized to help distinguish the insects' features.

Because the insects must hold very still, and be exposed to a good vacuum, all the insects I photographed with the SEM were dead. Or nearly dead, in the case of the clothes moth (page 27), which came back to life after having been doused with ether, coated with a thin layer of platinum (to increase electric conductivity), and photographed in the microscope's vacuum chamber. It even managed to escape from the specimen holder it had been glued to, meet a mate, and populate my entire apartment with its offspring, which ate some of my sofa. I am still amazed by the resilience of this tiny, fragile creature.

It is a particular challenge to photograph insects in action with an electron microscope, and I used a variety of tricks (from ether to shock freezing in liquid nitrogen) to get the shots in this book. The *Coenosia* fly eating the little fruit fly (page 89) is actually as dead as its prey; it was killed without causing it to drop its dinner. Soft, fragile insects also need to be completely dried to prevent shrinking when exposed to the vacuum. To do this, the water in the bug's bodies is gradually exchanged with chemicals that can evaporate without causing shrinking.

For insect portraiture, as for photographing people, the pose is all-important; soft tweezers and a very fine brush can help. But there is no way to manipulate two bugs into a photogenic pose together. Only patience, the sampling of many specimens, and luck can help here. The ants on page 17 started fighting on my desk while I was checking e-mail. They were from the same tribe, and so should not have been prone to tearing each other's antennae out. An entomologist told me that I had likely touched one with my fingers and my unbearable smell caused its sibling to attack it. I have no guess, however, as to why the lice (page 55) started to mate in the full light of my preparation microscope. Lice probably aren't shy, but biologically they should have been shy of the light. The mating ticks (page 65) found a cosier place for sex, hidden in the dense fur of a white Canadian shepherd dog. The female apparently didn't even bother to stop sucking the dog's blood during the act. But they were caught, both ending up in a vial and sent to me, still joined together, by a biologist (and dog owner).

Forensic entomology can be quite an upsetting business, but it is a field where bugs and humans meet intimately. To learn something about this, I enrolled in a course with Mark Benecke, a noted expert in the field. I was worried about having to dig up corpses of dead people in the name of science, but we actually created our own "criminal cases" by burying an assortment of dead pets supplied by a local vet (cats, guinea pigs, woodpeckers . . .) in the undergrowth of a municipal park in Cologne. When we came back to have a look at the marvellous insect collection that we hoped had made a home of these corpses, most of our animals were gone. Neighborhood dogs had found them in the undergrowth and retrieved them to their masters, showing total disrespect for the "experiment in progress" signs we had put up. The owners had, of course, put our specimens in the trash, which was then hauled away. Luckily, I was able to obtain some of the more common insects important to forensic entomology from other sources (*Calliphora* maggots, for instance, are good bait, and may be found in fishing shops).

Since smashed bugs on cars are also important in criminal investigations, I had to devise a way to photograph these poor traffic victims without scraping them off my windshield (and destroying the specimen in the process). By covering the front of my car with plastic wrap, I found that I could then simply cut a square of plastic around the bug to remove it intact. The amount of damage done to an insect is proportional to the speed of the car, so one should not go too fast to get good samples: The fly on page 120 I hit while traveling at about 45 mph in eastern France. May it serve as a memorial to all the bugs that are smashed without such noble recognition.

PAGE 134
Pogonomyrmex rugosus harvester ants scramble through the tunnels of their nest. They are the principal collectors and dispersers of seeds in semidesert landscapes of the southwestern United States and Mexico.

PAGE 135
Bert Hölldobler studies communications systems among *Camponotus sericeiventris* carpenter ants, which he has found lay trails by secreting a chemical from their hindguts.

LEFT
A pair of platinum-coated fighting *Camponotus floridanus* carpenter ants await immersion in the electron microscope.

BIBLIOGRAPHY

INTRODUCTION

Natalie Zemon Davis. *Women on the Margins: Three Seventeenth-Century Lives*. Cambridge: Harvard University Press, 1995.

Erich Hoyt and Ted Schultz, eds. *Insect Lives: Stories of Mystery and Romance from a Hidden World*. New York: John Wiley & Sons, Inc., 1999.

Franz Kafka. *Metamorphosis and Other Stories*. Translated by Willa and Edwin Muir. Harmondsworth, Middlesex: Penguin Books Ltd., 1961.

Herman Levinson and Anna Levinson. "Venerated beetles and their cultural-historical background in ancient Egypt." *Spixiana / Zeitschrift für Zoologie*, Supplement 27. Munich, 15 December 2001.

Jules Michelet. *The Insect*. With 140 Illustrations by Giacomelli. London: T. Nelson and Sons, Paternoster Row, 1883.

Vladimir Nabokov. *Nabokov's Butterflies: Unpublished and Uncollected Writings*. Edited and annotated by Brian Boyd and Robert Michael Pyle. New translations from the Russian by Dmitri Nabokov. Boston: Beacon Press, 2000.

Gilbert Waldbauer. *What Good Are Bugs? Insects in the Web of Life*. Cambridge: Harvard University Press, 2003.

HOME

Anonymous (c. 850). "Riddle/Bookworm." Translated from Anglo-Saxon by Edwin Morgan. Reprinted by permission of Carcanet Press, Ltd. from *Collected Translations*. Manchester: Carcanet Press, Ltd., 1996.

Charles T. Brues. *Insect Dietary: An Account of the Food Habits of Insects*. Cambridge: Harvard University Press, 1946.

Matthew Cobb. "Reading and writing The Book of Nature: Jan Swammerdam (1637–1680)." *Endeavour*, volume 24 (3) (2000): 122–128.

Walter Ebeling. *Urban Entomology*. Berkeley: University of California, 1978.

Arthur V. Evans and Charles L. Bellamy. *An Inordinate Fondness for Beetles*. Photography by Lisa Charles Watson. New York: Henry Holt and Company, 1996.

Karl von Frisch. *Ten Little Housemates*. London: Pergamon Press, 1960.

David George Gordon. *The Compleat Cockroach: A Comprehensive Guide to the Most Despised (and Least Understood) Creature on Earth*. Berkeley: Ten Speed Press, 1996.

Glenn W. Herrick. *Insects Injurious to the Household and Annoying to Man*. New York: The Macmillan Company, 1914.

Norman Hickin. *Bookworms: The Insect Pests of Books*. London: Sheppard Press Ltd., 1985.

Bert Hölldobler and Edward O. Wilson. *The Ants*. Cambridge: Harvard University Press, 1990.

Judith A. Holloway, et al. "Detection of house-dust-mite allergen in amniotic fluid and umbilical-cord blood," *The Lancet*, volume 356 (December 2, 2000): 1900–1902.

S. P. Hopkin, D. T. Jones and D. Dietrich. "The isopod *Porcellio scaber* as a monitor of the bioavailability of metals in terrestrial ecosystems: towards a global 'woodlouse watch' scheme." *The Science of the Total Environment*, Supplement 1993: 357–365.

Devin L. Jindrich and Robert J. Full. "Dynamic Stabilization of Rapid Hexapedal Locomotion." *The Journal of Experimental Biology* 205 (2002): 2803–2823.

Franz Kafka. *Metamorphosis and Other Stories*. Translated by Willa and Edwin Muir. Harmondsworth, Middlesex: Penguin Books, 1961.

Bernhard Klausnitzer. *Insects: Their Biology and Cultural History*. Photography by Manfred Förster. New York: Universe Books, 1987.

Gerald D. Schmidt, Larry S. Roberts and John Janovy, Jr. *Foundations of Parasitology*. Boston: McGraw Hill, 2000.

Henry David Thoreau. *Walden: or, Life in the Woods*. Boston: Ticknor and Fields, 1854.

Vincent B. Wigglesworth. *The Life of Insects*. Cleveland and New York: The World Publishing Company, 1964.

FOOD

Cyrus Abivardi. *Iranian Entomology: An Introduction*, volume 2. Berlin: Springer-Verlag, 2001.

House Dust Mite
enlarged 40,000%

Charles T. Brues. *Insect Dietary: An Account of the Food Habits of Insects.* Cambridge: Harvard University Press, 1946.

J. Henri Fabre. *The Life of the Grasshopper.* Translated by Alexander Teixera de Mattos. New York: Dodd, Mead and Company, 1920.

The Food Insects Newsletter. "Some Insect Foods of the American Indians: And How the Early Whites Reacted to Them." November 1994: Volume 7, Issue 3. *http://www.hollowtop.com/finl_html/amerindians.htm*

David George Gordon. *The Eat-A-Bug Cookbook.* Berkeley: Ten Speed Press, 1998.

Vincent M. Holt. *Why Not Eat Insects?* 1885. Reprint, Whitstable: Pryor Publications, 1992.

Hotlix
http://www.hotlix.com/
Tel. (805) 473-0596
Fax (805) 473-9074
P.O. Box 447, Grover Beach, CA 93433

H. Z. Levinson and A. R. Levinson. "Storage and insect species of stored grain and tombs in ancient Egypt." *Zeitschrift für Angewandte Entomologie* 100 (1985): 321–339.

Jules Michelet. *The Insect.* With 140 Illustrations by Giacomelli. London: T. Nelson and Sons, Paternoster Row, 1883.

Rumi. *Problem of Stinginess.* Translated by Cyrus Abivardi from Persian. N. Pour-Javadi, ed. *Mathnavi Ma'navi.* Tehran: Amir Kabir Publishing Institute, 1984. Reprinted by kind permission of Cyrus Abivardi and Springer-Verlag.

Peter Lund Simmonds. *The Curiosities of Food, or the Dainties and Delicacies of Different Nations Obtained from the Animal Kingdom.* 1859. Reprint with an introduction by Alan Davidson, Berkeley: Ten Speed Press, 2001.

Ronald Taylor and Barbara Carter. *Entertaining with Insects: The Original Guide to Insect Cookery.* Santa Barbara: Woodbridge Press Publishing Company, 1977.

U.S. Food and Drug Administration. The Food Defect Action Levels, May 1995; revised May 1998. *http://vm.cfsan.fda.gov/~dms/dalbook.html*

MEDICINE

William S. Baer. "The Treatment of Chronic Osteomyelitis with the Maggot (Larva of the Blow Fly)." *The Journal of Bone and Joint Surgery,* volume XIII, no. 3 (July 1931): 438-475.

Martin Brookes. *Fly: The Unsung Hero of Twentieth-Century Science.* New York: HarperCollins, 2001.

Norman F. Cantor. *In the Wake of the Plague: The Black Death and the World It Made.* New York: The Free Press, 2001.

J. L. Cloudsley-Thompson. *Insects and History.* New York: St. Martin's Press, 1976.

R. A. Cooper, P. C. Molan, and K. G. Harding. "The sensitivity to honey of Gram-positive cocci of clinical significance isolated from wounds." *Journal of Applied Microbiology,* volume 93 (2002): 857–863.

Valerie Curtis and Adam Biran. Dirt, "Disgust, and Disease: Is Hygiene in Our Genes?" *Perspectives in Biology and Medicine,* volume 44, No. 1 (Winter 2001): 17–31.

Howell V. Daly, John T. Doyen, and Alexander H. Purcell, III. *Introduction to Insect Biology and Diversity.* Oxford: Oxford University Press, second edition, 1998.

Charles Darwin. *The Voyage of the Beagle: Journal of Researches into the Natural History and Geology of the Countries Visited During the Voyage of H.M.S. Beagle Round the World.* New York: P. F. Collier & Son, 1909. Reprint, with introduction by Steve Jones, New York: Modern Library Paperback Edition, 2001.

Jerome Goddard. "Delusions of Parasitosis (Imaginary Insect or Mite Infestations)." In *Physician's Guide to Arthropods of Medical Importance,* 4th ed. Boca Raton: CRC Press, 2002.

Junitsu Ito, et al. "Transgenic anopheline mosquitos impaired in transmission of a malaria parasite." *Nature,* volume 417 (May 23, 2002): 452–455

Peter G. Kevan and Truman P. Phillips. "The Economic Impacts of Pollinator Declines: An Approach to Assessing the Consequences." *Conservation Ecology* 5 (1): 8 [online] *http://www.consecol.org/vol5/iss1/art8/*

Bernhard Klausnitzer. *Insects: Their Biology and Cultural History.* Photography by Manfred Förster. New York: Universe Books, 1987.

Body Louse
enlarged 5,000%

R. S. Lanciotti, et al. "Origin of the West Nile Virus Responsible for an Outbreak of Encephalitis in the Northeastern United States." *Science*, volume 286 (December 17, 1999) 2333–2337.

D. H. Lawrence, "The Mosquito." From *The Complete Poems of D. H. Lawrence*, Edited by V. de Sola Pinto and F. W. Roberts. Copyright © 1964, 1971 by Angelo Ravagli and C. M. Weekley, executors of the estate of Frieda Lawrence Ravagli. Used by permission of Viking Penguin, a division of Penguin Group (USA).

Guido Majno. *The Healing Hand: Man and Wound in the Ancient World*. Cambridge: Harvard University Press, 1975.

Anne Platt McGinn. "Malaria, Mosquitoes, and DDT: The toxic war against a global disease." *WorldWatch* (May/June 2002): 10–16.

Roger S. Nasci, et al. "West Nile Virus in Overwintering *Culex* Mosquitoes, New York City, 2000." *Emerging Infectious Diseases*, volume 7, no. 4 (July–August 2001): 742–744.

Christopher O'Toole, ed. *The Encyclopedia of Insects*. New York: Facts on File Publications, 1986.

A. B. Rich. *Our Near Neighbor the Mosquito*. New York: The Abbey Press, 1901.

Yibayiri O. Sanogo, et al. "*Bartonella henselae* in *Ixodes ricinus* Ticks (Acari: Ixodida) Removed from Humans, Belluno Province, Italy." *Emerging Infectious Diseases*, volume 9, no. 3 (March 2003): 329–332. ***http://www.cdc.gov/ncidod/ EID/vol9no3/02-0133.htm***

Gerald D. Schmidt, Larry S. Roberts and John Janovy, Jr. *Foundations of Parasitology*. Boston: McGraw Hill, 2000.

Stephen Trowell. "Drugs from Bugs: The Promise of Pharmaceutical Entomology." *The Futurist*, January–February 2003.

J.G. Valenzuela, et al. "Exploring the sialome of the tick *Ixodes scapularis*." *Journal of Experimental Biology*, volume 205 (2002): 2843–2864.

Hans Zinsser. *Rats, Lice and History. Being a Study in Biography, which, after Twelve Preliminary Chapters Indispensable for the Preparation of the Lay Reader, Deals with the Life History of TYPHUS FEVER*. Boston: printed and published for the Atlantic Monthly Press by Little, Brown and Company, 1935.

CONTROL

Andrew Beattie and Paul R. Ehrlich. *Wild Solutions: How Biodiversity is Money in the Bank*. New Haven: Yale University Press, 2001.

Association of Natural Biocontrol Producers: ***http://www.anbp.org/a-websites.htm***

May R. Berenbaum. *Bugs in the System: Insects and Their Impact on Human Affairs*. Cambridge: Perseus Books, 1995.

Rachel Carson. *Silent Spring*. Boston: Houghton Mifflin Company, 1962.

J. L. Cloudsley-Thompson. *Insects and History*. New York: St. Martin's Press, 1976.

Gustave P. Corten and Herman F. Veldkamp. "Insects can halve wind-turbine power." *Nature*, volume 412, (July 5, 2001): 41–42.

Gretchen C. Daily and Katherine Ellison. *The New Economy of Nature: The Quest to Make Conservation Profitable*. Washington: Island Press, 2002.

L. D. Foil and J. A. Hogsette. "Biology and control of tabanids, stable flies and horn flies." *Revue Scientifique et Technique-Office International des Epizooties*, volume 13 (4) (1994): 1125–1158.

Benjamin C. Garrett. "The Colorado Potato Beetle Goes to War." *Chemical Weapons Convention Bulletin: News, Background and Comment on Chemical and Biological Warfare Issues*. Quarterly Journal of the Harvard Sussex Program on CBW Armament and Arms Limitation. Issue No. 33 (September 1996).

Paul Hillyard. *The Book of the Spider: From Arachnophobia to the Love of Spiders*. New York: Random House, 1994.

L. O. Howard. *The Insect Menace*. New York: The Century Company, 1931.

Sue Hubbell. *Broadsides from the Other Orders: A Book of Bugs*. New York: Random House, 1993.

Claire Kremen, Neal M. Williams, and Robbin W. Thorp. Crop pollination from native bees at risk from agricultural intensification. *Proceedings of the National Academy of Sciences*, volume 99, no. 26 (December 24, 2002): 16812–16816. Online at ***http://www.pnas.org/cgi/doi/10.1073/pnas.262413599***

Larger Grain Borer
enlarged 6,000%

Primo Levi. *The Mirror Maker: Stories and Essays*. Translated from the Italian by Raymond Rosenthal. London: Abacus, 1997. (Originally published in Italian as Racconti e saggi, Turin: Editrice La Stampa s.p.a., 1986.)

Paul Mäder, et al. "Soil Fertility and Biodiversity in Organic Farming." *Science*, volume 296 (May 31, 2002): 1694-1697

Robert L. Metcalf and Robert A. Metcalf. *Destructive and Useful Insects: Their Habits and Control*, fifth edition. New York: McGraw Hill Inc., 1993.

E. W. Myers, et al. "A whole-genome assembly of *Drosophila*." *Science*, volume 287 (March 24, 2000): 2196-2204.

William S. Romoser and John G. Stoffolano, Jr. *The Science of Entomology*, fourth edition. Boston: McGraw-Hill, 1998.

J. Philip Spradbery. *Wasps: An Account of the Biology and Natural History of Solitary and Social Wasps*. Seattle: University of Washington Press, 1973.

Edwin Way Teale. *The Strange Lives of Familiar Insects*. New York: Dodd, Mead & Company, 1964.

Luther S. West. *The Housefly: Its Natural History, Medical Importance, and Control*. Ithaca, New York: Comstock Publishing Company, 1951.

CRIME

Gail S. Anderson. "Wildlife Forensic Entomology: Determining Time of Death in Two Illegally Killed Bear Cubs." *Journal of Forensic Sciences*, volume 44, (July 1999): 856-859.

Mark Benecke. "Six Forensic Entomology Cases: Description and Commentary." *Journal of Forensic Sciences*, volume 43, (1998): 797-805.

Dr. Zakaria Erzinçlioglu. *Maggots, Murder and Men: Memories and Reflections of a Forensic Entomologist*. Colchester: Harley Books, 2000.

M. Lee Goff. *A Fly for the Prosecution: How Insect Evidence Helps Solve Crimes*. Cambridge: Harvard University Press, 2000.

Miroslav Holub. *The Fly*. Translated from the Czech by George Theiner. From *Poems Before and After: Collected English Translations*. Miroslav Holub, Ian & Jarmila Milner (Translator), Ewald Osers (Translator), George Theiner (Translator) Highgreen, Northumberland: Bloodaxe Books Ltd., 1990. Reprinted by permission of Bloodaxe Books, Ltd.

Mark Hostetler. *That Gunk on Your Car: A Unique Guide to Insects of North America*. Berkeley: Ten Speed Press, 1997.

B. Thompson Lowne. *The Anatomy, Physiology, Morphology and Development of The Blow Fly. A Study in the Comparative Anatomy and Morphology of Insects*. London: R. H. Porter, 1890-92.

Eva Panagiotakopulu. "New Records for Ancient Pests: Archaeoentomology in Egypt." *Journal of Archaeological Science* volume 28 (2001): 1235-1246.

Jessica Snyder Sachs. *CORPSE: Nature, Forensics and the Struggle to Pinpoint Time of Death*. Cambridge: Perseus Publishing, 2001.

Karl Shapiro. "The Fly." In *Person, Place, and Thing*. New York: Reynal and Hitchcock, 1942. Reprinted in *Selected Poems by Karl Shapiro*, John Updike, ed. New York: Library of America, 2003.

Jeffrey D. Wells, et al. "Human and Insect Mitochondrial DNA Analysis from Maggots." *Journal of Forensic Sciences*, volume 46, no. 3 (2001): 685-687.

PETS

May R. Berenbaum. *Buzzwords: A Scientist Muses on Sex, Bugs, and Rock 'n' Roll*. Washington, D.C.: Joseph Henry Press, 2000.

Hans A. Hofmann and Paul A. Stevenson. "Flight restores fight in crickets." *Nature*, volume 403 (10 February 2000): 613.

Hans A. Hofmann and Klaus Schildberger. "Assessment of strength and willingness to fight during aggressive encounters in crickets." *Animal Behaviour*, volume 62 (2001): 337-348.

Brendan Lehane. *The Compleat Flea*. London: John Murray Ltd., 1969.

Sir John Lubbock. *Ants, Bees, and Wasps: A Record of Observations on the Habits of the Social Hymenoptera*. 1882. Reprinted by University Press of the Pacific, October 2001.

Sharman Apt Russell. *An Obsession with Butterflies: Our Long Love Affair with a Singular Insect*. Cambridge: Perseus Books, 2003.

Dylan Thomas. "Holiday Memory." First published in the volume *Quite Early One Morning*. London: J. M. Dent & Sons Ltd., 1954.

Red-shouldered Ham Beetle
enlarged 3,500%

aCKNOWLEDGMENTS

VOLKER STEGER

I would like to thank Bayer Environmental Science (Leverkusen), which is a fantastic source of pests; Judith Egelhof (Munich), who puts up with live bugs in the fridge; Josie Glausiusz (New York), who should write more books; Leonard Lessin (New York), who is a source of inspiration and encouragement; Monika Riedl (Stuttgart), of the Fraunhofer Institute IGB, who is a great SEM engineer; and Paul Stevenson (Leipzig), who makes crickets fight.

JOSIE GLAUSIUSZ

I would like to thank my parents, Irene and Gershon Glausiusz, for inspiring in me a love of the natural world and of my Jewish literary heritage; my grand-mother Amelia Harris, for unwavering love and steadfast faith in my talents; Michael Feinberg, for love, support and understanding; Philip Hobsbaum, for sage literary advice, keen encouragement and ever-stimulating debate on a fantastic variety of topics; to our agent Anne Depue; and of course, to Volker Steger, my collaborator and friend. It was a joy to work with you.

It is with grateful thanks that I acknowledge the input of the following scientists and others who promptly and kindly provided me with articles, references, data, and personal accounts of their encounters with insects:

INTRODUCTION
Professor Edward O. Wilson, Harvard University.

HOME
Mike Deutsch, Assured Environments, New York City; Robert Full, University of California, Berkeley; Steve Hopkin, University of Reading, U.K.; Carolyn Klass, Cornell University; Phil Koehler, University of Florida, Gainesville; Glen Needham, Ohio State University; David Pinniger, Consultant Entomologist, U.K.; and Jürgen Tautz, University of Würzburg, Germany.

FOOD
Cyrus Abivardi, Swiss Federal Institute of Technology (ETH), Zürich, Switzerland; Cornel Adler, Federal Biological Research Centre for Agriculture & Forestry, Berlin, Germany; David George Gordon; and Frank Ochmann, the chef at Soda, Berlin, Germany.

MEDICINE
Rose Cooper, University of Wales, Cardiff, U.K.; Valerie Curtis, London School of Hygiene and Tropical Medicine, U.K.; Jean-Luc Dimarcq, Entomed S.A., Illkirch, France; Wim Fleischmann, Bietigheim Clinic, Germany; Jerome Goddard, Mississippi Department of Health, Jackson, Mississippi; Roland Lupoli, Entomed S.A., Illkirch, France; Kosta Mumcuoglu, Hebrew University-Hadassah Medical School, Jerusalem, Israel; Roger Nasci, Centers for Disease Control and Prevention, Fort Collins, Colorado; Ronald Sherman, University of California, Irvine; Daniel Sonenshine, Old Dominion University, Norfolk, Virginia; Steve Thomas, Princess of Wales Hospital, Bridgend, U.K.; and Stephen Trowell, CSIRO Entomology, Canberra, Australia.

CONTROL
Jim Carpenter, American Museum of Natural History, New York; Gustave Corten, Energy Research Centre of the Netherlands; Gretchen Daily, Stanford University; Les Ehler, University of California, Davis; Angela Hale, The Bug Factory, Nanoose Bay, British Columbia, Canada; Blair Hedges, Pennsylvania State University; Jerry Hogsette, U.S. Department of Agriculture, Gainesville, Florida; Christian Nansen, Oklahoma State University; Linda Rayor, Cornell University; Ann Rypstra, Miami University, Ohio; Hans-Werner Schmidt, Bayer Environmental Science, Leverkusen, Germany; Jim Throne, U.S. Department of Agriculture, Manhattan, Kansas; and Barbara Tigar, Lancaster University, U.K.

CRIME
Gail Anderson, Simon Fraser University, British Columbia, Canada; Mark Benecke, International Forensic Research & Consulting, Cologne, Germany; Carlo P. Campobasso, Università di Bari, Italy; M. Lee Goff, Chaminade University, Honolulu, Hawaii; Mark Hostetler, University of Florida, Gainesville; and Jeffrey D. Wells, University of Alabama, Birmingham.

PETS
May Berenbaum, University of Illinois at Urbana-Champaign; and Paul Anthony Stevenson, University of Leipzig, Germany.

Cricket
enlarged 600%